Table of Contents

Preface

100 Words Every Middle Schooler Should Know has a simple purpose: to help you get to know 100 words that you are likely to come across in middle school. The words are useful and expressive ones, and you are sure to see them again and again as time goes on. Knowing these words will make it easier for you to understand what you read and will help you write more convincingly.

For each of the 100 words, we (the people who make *The American Heritage® Student Dictionary*) tell you how the word is pronounced, what it means, and where it comes from. We also explain what the different parts of the word mean, so you can see how these parts fit together. And we show you other words in English that are also made of these parts. For example, you will learn that the *-sist-* part of the word *persistent* goes back to Latin and means "stand." People who are persistent "keep standing," so to speak. They don't get knocked away from where they want to be. The word part *-sist-* also shows up in the verb *insist*, whose parts mean "stand on," that is, "not get away from something you are speaking about."

The 100 words themselves are taken from some of the books most often read in middle school English classes and from lists of favorites made by readers in grades 6 through 8. These books are part of a large body of literature and nonfiction titles written expressly for young people, but they are

100

WORDS every middle schooler should know

THE 100 WORDS® *From the Editors of the*
AMERICAN HERITAGE®
DICTIONARIES

HOUGHTON MIFFLIN HARCOURT
Boston   New York

EDITORIAL STAFF OF THE
American Heritage® Dictionaries

BRUCE NICHOLS, *Senior Vice President, Publisher, Adult Trade and Reference*

JOSEPH P. PICKETT, *Vice President, Executive Editor*

STEVEN R. KLEINEDLER, *Supervising Editor*

PATRICK TAYLOR, *Senior Lexicographer*

LOUISE E. ROBBINS, *Senior Editor*

SUSAN I. SPITZ, *Senior Editor*

CATHERINE T. PRATT, *Editor*

PETER CHIPMAN, *Associate Editor*

KATHERINE M. ISAACS, *Associate Editor*

Reading assistance provided by Adam Isaacs-Falbel and Rachel Isaacs-Falbel.

THE 100 WORDS ® is a registered trademark of
Houghton Mifflin Harcourt Publishing Company.

Visit our websites: ahdictionary.com
and hmhbooks.com

LIBRARY OF CONGRESS CATALOGING-IN-PUBLICATION DATA

100 words every middle schooler should know / from the editors of the American Heritage Dictionaries.

    p. cm. -- (100 words series)
  ISBN-13: 978-0-547-33322-9
  ISBN-10: 0-547-33322-6
  1. Vocabulary. I. Title: One hundred words every middle schooler should know.
  PE1449.A1456 2010
  428.1--dc22

                      2009050644

Text design by George Restrepo

MANUFACTURED IN THE UNITED STATES OF AMERICA

7 8 9 10 - EB - 15 14 13

enjoyed by many adults (including us). You've probably read books by some of these authors: Madeleine L'Engle, Russell Freedman, Neil Gaiman, Lois Lowry, Katherine Paterson, Philip Pullman, J. K. Rowling. They choose their words carefully, using them to imagine stories, to tell what happened in the past, and to explain how the world around us works.

Now you can start choosing your words carefully as well, following their lead.

Once you have gotten to know the words in *100 Words Every Middle Schooler Should Know,* you can challenge yourself further and learn more words by reading *100 Words Every High School Freshman Should Know,* and then after that *100 Words Every High School Graduate Should Know.*

You won't be sorry you learned all these words, and neither will your parents and teachers. Why not try it and see?

—Joseph P. Pickett
Executive Editor

Guide to the Entries

ENTRY WORDS The 100 words in this book are listed alphabetically. Each boldface entry word is followed by its pronunciation (see page ix for a pronunciation key) and at least one part of speech. One or more definitions are given for each part of speech with the central and most commonly sought sense first.

QUOTATIONS Each definition is followed by quotations from fiction and nonfiction to show the word in context. The order of the quotations corresponds to the order of senses presented.

WORD ORIGINS Every word in this book is accompanied by a paragraph explaining the origin of the word. The paragraphs usually trace the word back to Latin, Greek, or other ancient languages. The Word Origins also discuss how words in English and other languages can be broken down into their constituent parts, in order to help middle schoolers remember the meanings of new words easily and make these words part of their active vocabulary. Most of the words in this book are from Latin, the language of the Roman Empire, and many of these Latin words are compounds that can be broken down into simpler elements that can be remembered easily. Other words discussed in this book are from ancient Greek (as opposed to its modern-day descendant, the spoken language of modern Greece). The Word Origin notes also refer to a few other languages and linguistic terms that may not be familiar to the average reader but are essential for understanding the history of English.

Old French refers to the French language as it was spoken and written from about 800 (the time of the first documents written in French) to about 1500.

The term *Germanic* refers to languages belonging to the family of languages that includes English and its close relatives Dutch, German, Danish, Icelandic, Norwegian, and Swedish.

The term *Old English* refers to the English language as spoken from about the middle of the 400s to around 1150. (The Anglo-Saxons began to settle in England and establish their Germanic language, the ancestor of Modern English, in the middle of the 400s.)

Middle English refers to the English language as spoken from about 1150 to 1500, between the Old English and Modern English periods.

Modern English refers to English as it was spoken and written since about 1500.

Old Norse refers to the Germanic language of Iceland and Scandinavia until about 1350. The different regional varieties of Old Norse evolved into Icelandic, Danish, Norwegian, and Swedish. Old Norse was also spoken by the Vikings who settled in Scotland and the northern part of England in the Middle Ages. During the Old English period, English borrowed many words from Old Norse spoken by these Viking settlers.

Pronunciation Guide

Pronunciations appear in parentheses after boldface entry words. If a word has more than one pronunciation, the first pronunciation is usually more common than the other, but often they are equally common. Pronunciations are shown after inflections and related words where necessary.

Stress is the relative degree of emphasis that a word's syllables are spoken with. An unmarked syllable has the weakest stress in the word. The strongest, or primary, stress is indicated with a bold mark (ʹ). A lighter mark (ʹ) indicates a secondary level of stress. The stress mark follows the syllable it applies to. Words of one syllable have no stress mark because there is no other stress level that the syllable can be compared to.

The key on page ix shows the pronunciation symbols used in this book. To the right of the symbols are words that show how the symbols are pronounced. The letters whose sound corresponds to the symbols are shown in boldface.

The symbol (ə) is called *schwa*. It represents a vowel with the weakest level of stress in a word. The schwa sound varies slightly according to the vowel it represents or the sounds around it:

a·bun·dant (ə-bŭnʹdənt)   **mo·ment** (mōʹmənt)
civ·il (sĭvʹəl)   **grate·ful** (grātʹfəl)

PRONUNCIATION KEY

Symbol	Examples	Symbol	Examples
ă	pat	oi	noise
ā	pay	ŏŏ	took
âr	care	ŏŏr	lure
ä	father	ōō	boot
b	bib	ou	out
ch	church	p	pop
d	deed, milled	r	roar
ĕ	pet	s	sauce
ē	bee	sh	ship, dish
f	fife, phase,	t	tight, stopped
	rough	th	thin
g	gag	*th*	this
h	hat	ŭ	cut
hw	which	ûr	urge, term,
ĭ	pit		firm, word,
ī	pie, by		heard
îr	deer, pier	v	valve
j	judge	w	with
k	kick, cat, pique	y	yes
l	lid, needle	z	zebra, xylem
m	mum	zh	vision,
n	no, sudden		pleasure,
ng	thing		garage
ŏ	pot	ə	about, item,
ō	toe		edible,
ô	caught,		gallop,
	paw		circus
ôr	core	ər	butter

". . . you are, I believe, complete novices in the use of nonverbal spells. What is the advantage of a nonverbal spell?"

Hermione's hand shot into the air. Snape took his time looking around at everybody else, making sure he had no choice, before saying curtly, "Very well—Miss Granger?"

"Your **adversary** has no warning about what kind of magic you're about to perform," said Hermione, "which gives you a split-second advantage."

—J. K. Rowling, *Harry Potter and the Half-Blood Prince*

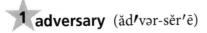

1 adversary (ăd**ʹ**vər-sĕr**ʹ**ē)

noun

An opponent or enemy.

> I saw no need to tell him about my letter to my brother. Abraham has always told me that the less you let an **adversary** know about you, the better off you'll be. And something told me Benjamin Fishbourne was an **adversary**.
>
> —Ann Rinaldi, *A Ride into Morning: The Story of Tempe Wick*

> WORD ORIGIN *Adversary* comes from Latin *adversārius,* meaning "enemy." *Adversārius* itself was made from the Latin adjective *adversus,* meaning "against, opposite." An adversary is "one who is against another." Other English words that come from Latin *adversus* are *adverse,* "unfavorable," and *adversity,* "hardship."

2 aplomb (ə-plŏm′ *or* ə-plŭm′)

noun

Self-confidence, especially in a difficult situation; poise; assurance.

> She stood behind the tree and watched them walk toward the house. Then a *really* funny thing happened. Mr. Waldenstein got on his bicycle. Harriet thought for a minute that he was going off for a while to deliver things, but then her hair stood on end as she watched Ole Golly, with great agility and even more **aplomb**, hop onto the delivery cart.
>
> —Louise Fitzhugh, *Harriet the Spy*

WORD ORIGIN *Aplomb* comes from the French word *aplomb,* which means basically "vertical position" and also "stability" and "emotional control under pressure." French *aplomb* comes from the phrase *à plomb,* meaning "exactly vertical, perpendicular to the ground." This phrase is made up of the preposition *à,* meaning "to" and "according to," and *plomb,* meaning "(the metal) lead" or "lead weight." Builders and engineers often need to find out whether an object is perfectly upright or not, and they can do this by suspending a heavy lead weight at the end of a cord and using it to determine which direction is straight down.

---

3 apprehensive (ăp′rĭ-hĕn′sĭv)

adjective

Anxious or fearful; uneasy.

> Maroo was **apprehensive**, not only at the prospect of lead-
> ing the journey, but also at the thought of controlling Otak.
> Would he obey her?
>
> —Ann Turnbull, *Maroo of the Winter Caves*

WORD ORIGIN The original meaning of *apprehensive* in English was "seizing upon something
(such as a new idea) quickly or firmly." Nowadays
apprehensive is more often used to describe people
who seize upon, that is, think or worry about, any
slight sign of danger or disturbance. *Apprehensive*
comes from the Latin verb *apprehendere*, "to seize."
Apprehendere is also the source of English *appre-
hend*.

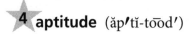

4 aptitude (ăp′tĭ-tōōd′)

noun

The ability to learn or understand something quickly.

> She began to describe this year's group and its variety of personalities, though she singled no one out by name. She mentioned that there was one who had singular skills at caretaking, another who loved newchildren, one with unusual scientific **aptitude**, and a fourth for whom physical labor was an obvious pleasure.
>
> —Lois Lowry, *The Giver*

WORD ORIGIN *Aptitude* comes from Latin *aptitūdō*, meaning "aptitude." *Aptitūdō* in turn comes from Latin *aptus*, meaning "ready" and "suitable or fit for a purpose." Aptitude is "suitability for doing a task." *Aptus* is also the source of the English word *apt*, "exactly suitable."

5 attentive (ə-tĕn′tĭv)

adjective

1. Giving attention to something. **2.** Paying careful attention to the comfort or concerns of others; considerate.

> Without further delay, Taran lifted Kaw from his fireside perch and carried him to the dooryard. This time the crow did not clack his beak or gabble impudently. Instead of his customary scoldings, hoarse quackings, and mischievous foolery, Kaw hunched on Taran's wrist and cocked a beady, **attentive** eye, listening closely while Taran carefully explained the task.
>
> —Lloyd Alexander, *The High King*

> He looked as dry as dust and no more kindly than a silver ink-pot, but he was as polite and **attentive** to those two little girls as if they'd been the Duchess of Savoy and her twin sister.
>
> —Philip Pullman, *Count Karlstein*

WORD ORIGIN *Attentive* comes from Latin *attentus,* "attentive." *Attentus* comes from the Latin verb *attendō,* "to listen carefully, pay attention." *Attendō* is also the source of English *attend* and *attention.*

6 banish (băn′ĭsh)

verb

To force to leave a country or place; exile.

> I do not know whether Father Linares saw it again or not, but I do know that while it lived there in the sea it lost the claws and forked tongue and the evil smell. It became the most beautiful creature I have ever seen. Yes, beautiful. And still it was the same evil thing that Father Linares **banished** from our land many years ago. This is strange.
>
> —Scott O'Dell, *The Black Pearl*

WORD ORIGIN *Banish* comes from the medieval French verb *banir,* "to banish." *Banir* comes from the medieval French noun *ban,* "proclamation." In medieval times, a person was banished by the public announcement of the authorities. The French word *ban* is related to the English word *ban* meaning "to prohibit" and "prohibition."

7 barricade (băr′ĭ-kād′)

noun

1. A usually temporary structure set up, as across a route of access, to block the passage of an enemy or opponent. **2.** Something that serves as an obstacle; a barrier.

verb

1. To block an opening or passage with an obstacle or a barrier. **2.** To enclose or exclude someone by constructing a barricade.

There are people in this world who are naturally open and easy to get to know, and there are difficult people, the ones who put up **barricades** and expect you to climb over them.

—Janet Taylor Lisle, *The Art of Keeping Cool*

Gracie was happy to have the owl back in the eaves. It added zest and youth to her life to have something to watch again as she basked in the blazing sunshine. And it was interesting to watch Pinky's energetic attempts to open up the little door, which was too well **barricaded** with a stout board for her to succeed.

—Eleanor Estes, *Pinky Pye*

When I carried up a basin of warm water I discovered that Juan had **barricaded** himself in. There were no fastenings on the doors, but he had dragged (with strength obtained from heaven knows where) a bench across the room so as to bar the door.

—Joan Aiken, *Bridle the Wind*

WORD ORIGIN *Barricade* comes from the French word *barricade,* "a barricade." French *barricade* in turn comes from the French noun *barrique,* "large wooden barrel." Barricades were often used to block streets in Paris during clashes between Catholics and Protestants in the 1500s, and these barricades were made from wine barrels filled with earth or stones. News of the struggles in Paris reached England and helped to make the word *barricade* well known in English.

8 bluff (blŭf)

verb

To engage in a false display of strength or confidence, especially in order to deceive someone.

> A full minute went by before it dawned on me that I was still in one piece. When I realized this, I began noticing things. Every time the big monkey ran at me he only came a little way, then he would turn and shuffle back. He was **bluffing**.
>
> —Wilson Rawls, *Summer of the Monkeys*

WORD ORIGIN *Bluff* comes from Dutch *bluffen*, "to brag." Dutch *bluffen* may be related to the Dutch word *blaffen*, "to yelp, to insult someone with calls or shouts," and to the German word *blaffen*, "to yelp."

9 brackish (brăk′ĭsh)

adjective

Slightly salty.

In my nostrils, the faint hay smell of the grass mingled with that of the **brackish** water of the Bay, while the spring wind chilled the tips of my ears and raised goosebumps along my arms.

—Katherine Paterson, *Jacob Have I Loved*

WORD ORIGIN From the late middle ages to the 1700s, ports in the Netherlands and northern Germany were important shipping centers. Sailors and merchants from these regions often met and worked with their counterparts from England and Scotland. As a result of these contacts, English borrowed many words relating to seafaring and the sea from languages spoken in these parts of Europe.

Brackish, for example, comes from Low German *brack,* "brackish water." Low German is the language spoken by many people in everyday life in the northern part of Germany. It is different from— but closely related to—the standard German language taught in schools in Germany. Each area in Germany has its own variety of German that can often be difficult to understand for Germans not from that area. Low German is called *low* not because it is crude or vulgar, but because the land in northern Germany where it is spoken is low, near sea level.

10 brandish (brăn′dĭsh)

verb

To wave or exhibit something in a dramatic or threatening way.

> "Allow me!" shouted Lockhart. He **brandished** his wand at the snake and there was a loud bang; the snake, instead of vanishing, flew ten feet into the air and fell back to the floor with a loud smack.
>
> —J. K. Rowling, *Harry Potter and the Chamber of Secrets*

WORD ORIGIN *Brandish* comes from the Old French verb *brandir,* "to brandish." French *brandir* in turn was made from the Old French noun *brand,* "sword." The French language got this word from the Franks, a people speaking a Germanic language who conquered France as the Roman Empire began to break apart in the 400s. This Frankish word is related to the English word *brand* that means basically "a burning piece of wood" and "a piece of iron heated in order to burn a mark."

In poetry, English *brand* is sometimes used with the meaning "a sword" just like the French word *brand*. However, the original meaning of the Frankish word was probably "a torch or burning piece of wood" or "something that glows like a torch"—when a sword is brandished, it is held up like a torch and it can flash in the sunlight. The common modern meaning of English *brand*, "a name that identifies a product," comes from the fact that certain kinds of commercial goods or containers once had identifying marks burned into them.

At this moment her thoughts were interrupted by a loud shouting of "Ahoy! Ahoy! Check!" and a Knight, dressed in crimson armor, came galloping down upon her, **brandishing** a great club. Just as he reached her, the horse stopped suddenly: "You're my prisoner!" the Knight cried, as he tumbled off his horse.

—Lewis Carroll, *Through the Looking-Glass*

11 circumference (sər-kŭm′fər-əns)

noun

The boundary of an area, an object, or a geometric figure, especially a circle.

"Do you always travel that way?" asked Milo as he glanced curiously at the strange circular room, whose sixteen tiny arched windows corresponded exactly to the sixteen points of the compass. Around the entire **circumference** were numbers from zero to three hundred and sixty, marking the degrees of the circle, and on the floor, walls, tables, chairs, desks, cabinets, and ceiling were labels showing their heights, widths, depths, and distances to and from each other.

—Norton Juster, *The Phantom Tollbooth*

WORD ORIGIN *Circumference* comes from the Latin word *circumferentia,* meaning "circumference." This Latin word originally referred to the circular course traced by mathematicians using a compass (the instrument consisting of two legs hinged together used to draw circles). *Circumferentia* itself was made from the Latin word *circumferre,* meaning "to carry around in a circle, trace a circular course." The circumference of a circle is in origin "the circular course traced by a compass or other instrument."

The Latin word *circumferre* is made up of *circum,* "around," and *ferre,* "to carry." Latin *circum* can also be found in many other English words of Latin origin that relate to the notion of "being around," such as *circumlocution,* "talking around a subject rather than stating it directly," *circumpolar,* "lying around the earth's poles," *circumstance,* "the conditions existing around an event," and *circumvent,* "to avoid by going around."

12 commotion (kə-mō′shən)

noun

Noisy activity or confusion.

> The day whizzed by, and so did his afternoon chores and dinner. Suddenly he was dressed in his best clothes and standing next to Benny backstage, listening to the **commotion** as the cafeteria filled with school kids and parents.
>
> —Gary Soto, "La Bamba," *Baseball in April and Other Stories*

WORD ORIGIN *Commotion* comes from the Latin word *commōtiō*, "commotion." *Commōtiō* is made from the Latin verb *commovēre*, "to move vigorously, shake up." *Commovēre* is made up of the Latin prefix *com-*, which strengthens the meanings of verbs, and *movēre*, "to move." *Movēre* is also the source of the English words *move* and *motion.*

13 concoction (kən-kŏk′shən)

noun

Something that has been prepared by putting several things together; a mixture of ingredients.

> In their pine-bough snow enclosure, with a crackling fire before them, they ate from their sack of dried meat and drank the **concoction** of strengthening swamp tea leaves that Nokomis had plucked from bushes as they walked.
>
> —Louise Erdrich, *The Porcupine Year*

WORD ORIGIN *Concoction* comes from the Latin verb *concoquere,* "to cook, boil down, concoct a poison." This Latin verb is made up of the prefix *com-* (which becomes *con-* before certain consonants), meaning "completely, thoroughly," and the verb *coquere,* meaning simply "to cook." Both the English noun *cook* and the English verb *to cook* come from the Latin noun *coquus,* "a cook," which is related to the Latin verb *coquere.*

★ 14 conspicuous (kən-spĭk′yōō-əs)

adjective

1. Easily seen; obvious. **2.** Attracting attention; striking; remarkable.

> The fifth-grade boys, bursting with new importance, ordered the fourth graders this way and that, while the smaller boys tried to include themselves without being **conspicuous**.
>
> —Katherine Paterson, *Bridge to Terabithia*

> Wherever Tom and Huck appeared they were courted, admired, stared at. The boys were not able to remember that their remarks had possessed weight before; but now their sayings were treasured and repeated; everything they did seemed somehow to be regarded as remarkable; they had evidently lost the power of doing and saying commonplace things; moreover, their past history was raked up and discovered to bear marks of **conspicuous** originality.
>
> —Mark Twain, *The Adventures of Tom Sawyer*

WORD ORIGIN *Conspicuous* comes from the Latin adjective *cōnspicuus,* meaning "conspicuous." *Cōnspicuus* itself comes from the Latin verb *cōnspicere,* "to notice, catch sight of." This Latin verb is made up of the prefix *com-* (which becomes *cōn-* before certain consonants), meaning "completely, thoroughly," and the verb *specere,* meaning "to see, to observe." The Latin verb *specere* is also the source of many other English words such as *perspective,* "way of seeing things," *spectacle,* "event worth seeing," and *spectator,* "one who sees an event."

⭐ 15 contortion (kən-tôr′shən)

noun

A sharp twist or bend in something.

> If you look at old pictures in the *Two Mills Times*, you see that the Knot was about the size and shape of a lopsided volleyball. It was made of string, but it had more **contortions**, ins and outs, twists and turns and dips and doodles than the brain of Albert Einstein himself.
>
> —Jerry Spinelli, *Maniac Magee*

🍃 WORD ORIGIN *Contortion* comes from the Latin noun *contortiō*, meaning "twisting around." *Contortiō* itself comes from the Latin verb *contorquere*, "to twist." This Latin verb is made up of the prefix *com-* (which becomes *con-* before certain consonants), meaning "together" or "completely," and the verb *torquere*, meaning "to twist." The Latin verb *torquere* is also the source of many other English words relating to twisting or circular movement, such as *distort*, "to twist out of shape," *torque*, "a force that causes an object to rotate around an axis," and *torture*, "twisting a person's body to cause pain."

16 counter (koun′tər)

verb

To do or say something in opposition to something else.

> Claudia, who had eaten cereal and drunk pineapple juice, scolded him about the need to eat properly. Breakfast food for breakfast, and lunch food for lunch. Jamie **countered** with complaints about Claudia's narrow-mindedness.
>
> —E. L. Konigsburg, *From the Mixed-up Files of Mrs. Basil E. Frankweiler*

WORD ORIGIN *Counter* comes from the Old French preposition *contre*, "against." The Old French word in turn comes from Latin *contrā*, "against." The Latin preposition *contrā* can be found in many other words relating to the concept of being opposite or opposed to something, such as *contradict*, "to say something that goes against what another says," and *contrary*, "opposing."

⭐17 cunning (kŭn′ĭng)

adjective

Sly, crafty, or clever.

noun

The quality of being sly, crafty, or clever.

> Not that his whole year at Hogwarts had been fun. At the very end of last term, Harry had come face-to-face with none other than Lord Voldemort himself. Voldemort might be a ruin of his former self, but he was still terrifying, still **cunning**, still determined to regain power.
>
> —J. K. Rowling, *Harry Potter and the Chamber of Secrets*

> His **cunning** was wolf **cunning**, and wild **cunning**; his intelligence, shepherd intelligence and St. Bernard intelligence; and all this, plus an experience gained in the fiercest of schools, made him as formidable a creature as any that roamed the wild.
>
> —Jack London, *The Call of the Wild*

🍁 WORD ORIGIN The original meaning of the auxiliary verb *can* in Old English was "to know." If you *know* how to do something, you *can* do it. The auxiliary verb *can* also used to have more principal parts in Old English and Middle English that it has now in Modern English. For example, *can* had an infinitive spelled *cunnan* that meant "to know, to be able to do." Nowadays, most of these other principal parts of the verb *can* have fallen out of use. However, *can* also had a present participle, *cunning*, that meant "knowing how to do something"—this word has survived in Modern English as the adjective *cunning*, meaning "sly, crafty, or clever."

---

18 debris (də-brēʹ)

noun

The scattered remains of something broken, destroyed, or discarded; rubble or wreckage.

> There was a shadowy alcove at the other end of the cellar, filled with old furniture and other stuff. Adam recognized old wicker chairs they had used long ago in the summer, in the backyard. His mother waded through this **debris** of other years, clearing a path to a box tied with an old rope, about four feet square, in the corner.
>
> —Robert Cormier, *I Am the Cheese*

> WORD ORIGIN *Debris* comes from the French noun *débris,* meaning "debris." This French word comes from the Old French verb *debrisier,* "to break to pieces," made up of the French prefix *de-* (which strengthens the meaning of verbs) and the Old French verb *brisier,* "to break."

19 defiance (dĭ-fīʹəns)

noun

The act of defying; open resistance to an opposing force or authority.

> The name of Gessler seemed to make Tell even more rebellious. He laughed in **defiance**, as Walter clung to him and shrank back from the lowered spears of the soldiers.
>
> —Mary and Conrad Buff, *The Apple and the Arrow*

20 deft (dĕft)

adjective

Quick and skillful; adroit.

> In Arbois, Louis worked hard—drawing pastel portraits of his parents, the mayor, a nun, a barrel maker, and other local citizens. Would he have become a renowned artist if he had chosen to continue drawing instead of studying chemistry? Some critics find marks of artistic talent in the pastels; others think they display little creativity. What they certainly show, however, are qualities of observation, attention to detail, and a **deft** hand that served him well in the laboratory.
>
> —Louise E. Robbins, *Louis Pasteur and the Hidden World of Microbes*

WORD ORIGIN *Deft* comes from the Middle English word *deft*, which could mean both "humble" and "skillful." The original link between these two different meanings of *deft*, "humble" and "skillful," was probably the notion of "acting appropriately for the circumstances." In origin, *deft* is probably just a slightly changed pronunciation of the Middle English word *daft*, "humble, meek." Eventually, the spelling *deft* came to be thought of as a different word (meaning "skillful") from *daft* (meaning "humble"). Middle English *daft*, "humble," then developed a range of other meanings, including "innocent" and "simple-minded, foolish." Today, *daft* usually means "crazy." The word *daffy*, "crazy," is probably related to *deft* and *daft*.

21 destination (dĕs′tə-nā′shən)

noun

The place to which a person or thing is going or is sent.

> The train had left the levels and was running into more upland country—waste, wide, and lonely, with not a living thing stirring across its bare and open expanses. It was bleak and forbidding, and Sylvia shivered a little, thinking what a long way there was yet to go before she reached her unknown **destination**.
>
> —Joan Aiken, *The Wolves of Willoughby Chase*

WORD ORIGIN *Destination* comes from the Latin noun *dēstinātiō*, meaning "a determination, a purpose." A destination is the determined point at which a journey ends. Latin *dēstinātiō* comes from the Latin verb *dēstināre*, "to decide firmly to do something, resolve, determine." Latin *dēstināre* is also the source of English *destine* and *destiny*.

⭐22 diminish (dĭ-mĭn′ĭsh)

verb

To make or become smaller or less; reduce or decrease.

Will blew out his cheeks and set off to climb the staircase. It was made of blackened oak, immense and broad, with steps as worn as the flagstones: far too solid to creak underfoot. The light **diminished** as they climbed, because the only illumination was the small deep-set window on each landing.

—Philip Pullman, *The Subtle Knife*

WORD ORIGIN *Diminish* has a complicated history. It developed from a blending of two medieval English verbs, *diminuen* and *minishen*. *Diminuen*, meaning "to lessen," comes from Latin *dēminuere*, "to lessen." *Dēminuere* itself is a compound of the prefix *dē-*, meaning "off, away," and *minuere*, "to make smaller, lessen." *Minishen*, "to reduce," comes from Latin *minūtus*, "made smaller, lessened," which is the past participle of *minuere*. In this way, both medieval English verbs ultimately come from Latin *minuere*, "to make smaller." Other English words from Latin that belong to this family of words are the adjective *minute*, "very small," and the noun *minute*, "a sixtieth of an hour (that is, a small bit of an hour)."

He wanted to stay near the lake because he thought the plane, even deep in the water, might show up to somebody flying over and he didn't want to **diminish** any chance he might have of being found.

—Gary Paulsen, *Hatchet*

23 disdain (dĭs-dān′)

noun

A feeling that someone or something is bad, worthless, or low; scorn or contempt.

verb

To have or show this feeling about someone or something.

> There was plenty of bread left on the table, but it was sliced bakery bread from the Camerons' shop, wrapped in plastic, and the Boggart looked at it with **disdain**. Compared to the wonderful coarse wholemeal bread the MacDevon had baked once a week, this was poor stuff.
>
> —Susan Cooper, *The Boggart*

> She **disdained** them for being so stupid and boring and uninterested in anything important, like the Great Depression, or the British in India, or poetry, or ballet, or anything—except each other.
>
> —Zilpha Keatley Snyder, *Libby on Wednesday*

WORD ORIGIN *Disdain* comes from the Old French verb *desdeignier,* meaning "to disdain." This French verb comes from the Latin verb *dēdignārī,* made up of the Latin prefix *dē-,* "off, away," added to the Latin verb *dignārī,* "to deem worthy." *Dignārī* itself comes from the Latin adjective *dignus,* "worthy." Other English words that come from *dignus* are *dignity,* "the quality of being worthy of respect," and *dignify,* "to make worthy of respect."

Thick clumps of yellow and deep pink flowers fringed the edge of the small dwelling with its hand-hewn beams and thatched roof. Matty had never paid attention to the names of flowers—boys generally **disdained** such things—but now he wished he knew them, so that he could tell Jean.

—Lois Lowry, *Messenger*

24 dismal (dĭz′məl)

adjective

1. Causing gloom or depression; dreary. **2.** Feeling gloomy; depressed; miserable.

> The farms were not nearly so well cared for here as they were farther back. There were fewer houses and fewer fruit trees, and the farther they went the more **dismal** and lonesome the country became.
>
> —L. Frank Baum, *The Wonderful Wizard of Oz*

> All the stories of ghosts and goblins that he had heard in the afternoon, now came crowding upon his recollection. The night grew darker and darker; the stars seemed to sink deeper in the sky, and driving clouds occasionally hid them from his sight. He had never felt so lonely and **dismal**.
>
> —Washington Irving, *The Legend of Sleepy Hollow*

WORD ORIGIN For many of us Monday is *dismal*, a bad day. In fact, the English word *dismal* comes from the Old French phrase *dis mal*, literally meaning "bad days." This phrase originally referred to two days each month that were unlucky according to medieval belief. For instance, the first and the fourth of January and the fourth and the twenty-sixth of February were considered unlucky. Those English speakers who didn't understand French spoke of *dismal days*, not realizing that this literally meant "bad days days." Eventually English *dismal* came to be an adjective meaning "bad, unlucky." Any venture begun on one of these dismal days, it was believed, had dismal prospects.

⭐ 25 dispel (dĭ-spĕl′)

verb

To cause to disappear; drive away; disperse.

> From the threshold, I saw the glow of the railroad lantern. A fire burned in the little stove, warming the air slightly but not enough to **dispel** the odor of kerosene, damp earth, and old wool.
>
> —Mary Downing Hahn, *Stepping on the Cracks*

🍁 WORD ORIGIN *Dispel* comes from the Latin verb *dispellere*. *Dispellere* is a compound made up of the Latin prefix *dis-*, meaning "apart, in separate directions," added to the verb *pellere*, "to set in motion, drive." When you dispel someone's fears, you drive them away, so to speak.

★26 eavesdrop (ēvz′drŏp′)

verb

To listen secretly to the private conversation of others.

> He and Mom went outside after supper and sat on the swing. I could hear murmured conversation from them, but I didn't try to **eavesdrop**.
>
> —Susan Beth Pfeffer, *Life As We Knew It*

🔸 WORD ORIGIN The edge of the roof that overhangs the side of a building is the *eaves*, and an *eavesdrop* is the space on the ground where the rainwater falls from the eaves. If you stood in the eavesdrop by a window on the side of a building to listen secretly to a conversation inside, you were said to be *eavesdropping*. The meaning of *eavesdrop* has broadened so that now you can eavesdrop anywhere.

★27 egregious (ĭ-grē′jəs)

adjective

Well beyond the bounds of what is right or proper; outrageous.

> "We, the fourteen members of the Mouse Council, have discussed your behavior. First, we will give you a chance to defend yourself against these rumors of your **egregious** acts. Did you or did you not sit at the foot of the human king?"
>
> —Kate DiCamillo, *The Tale of Despereaux*

🔸 WORD ORIGIN *Egregious* comes from Latin *ēgregius*, "standing out." Latin *ēgregius* itself is made up of the Latin prefix ē- (the form that the prefix *ex-*, "out," takes before certain consonants), and *greg-*, a form of the Latin word *grex*, "herd." So something that is egregious is like an animal that stands away from the herd. The Latin word *grex* is also the source of the English word *gregarious*, used to describe people who seek out and enjoy the company of others.

28 ember (ĕm′bər)

noun

A glowing piece of burning wood or coal.

The barn's loft held over three tons of timothy hay, delivered earlier that day. Flames from the burning hay pushed against the roof and beams, almost as if they were struggling to break free. A shower of burning **embers** greeted Sullivan as he entered the building.
— Jim Murphy, *The Great Fire*

WORD ORIGIN *Ember* is a very old Germanic word, reflecting the traditional importance of the hearth in ancient households. The hearth was where the cooking was done and people warmed themselves. The English word *ember* is related to the German word *Ammern*, "embers," and the Old Norse word *eimyrja*, "ember." In writings from Middle English times, the word was originally spelled *emere*, but the *e* in the middle of the word was often dropped. This would have caused the *m* and the *r* to come together and make the difficult-to-pronounce word *emre*. However, a *b* was inserted into the consonant cluster *mr* to make it easier to say, and the word became *embre* in Middle English and eventually *ember* in Modern English.

The Egg was perfectly still for a few more minutes, and then it jerked. A hairline crack appeared on the top. Nothing else happened for what seemed a very long time, and then the Egg really began to move. It quivered, tilted, and rolled over. The crack lengthened, widened, and a tiny beak **emerged** at the top.

—Luli Gray, *Falcon's Egg*

29 emerge (ĭ-mûrj′)

verb

To become visible or known.

> Serafina listened as he told her of the rumors that had swept the town. Amid the fog of rumor, a few facts had begun to **emerge** clearly.
>
> —Philip Pullman, *The Subtle Knife*

WORD ORIGIN *Emerge* comes from Latin *ēmergere*, "to emerge." *Ēmergere* itself is a compound of *ē-*, a form of the Latin prefix *ex-*, meaning "out of," and *mergere*, "to dip, plunge, sink." So something that emerges is like something that comes out of the water. Latin *mergere* is also the source of the English word *submerge*, "to put under water."

30 engross (ĕn-grōs′)

verb

To occupy the complete attention of someone; absorb.

He began wandering around the room, picking things up and putting them down again. "Where's your TV?" he asked after a while. She pretended to be too **engrossed** in her reading to hear. "I *said* where's your TV?"

—Stephanie S. Tolan, *Surviving the Applewhites*

WORD ORIGIN The earlier meaning of *engross* in English was "to buy up in large quantities, to monopolize." An *engrossing* book monopolizes your attention, so to speak. The English word *engross* comes from the medieval French verb *engrossier*, "to buy up in large quantities." The French verb itself comes from the phrase *en gros*, "in large quantities." *En* in French means "in," and *gros* means "large." French *gros* is also the source of the English word *gross*. The original meaning of *gross* is "large, thick," but *gross* has also come to mean "unrefined, crude," and—in slang—simply "disgusting." In this way, the *-gross-* in *engross* has the same origin as the slang word often heard as the exclamation *Gross!*

⭐ 31 exasperation (ĭg-zăs′pə-rā′shən)

noun

A state of anger, impatience, or great irritation.

> Upon seeing the wet, dirtied cashmere sweater—twigs and weeds sprouting from the sleeves—Floy threw her arms up in **exasperation**.
>
> —Kevin Henkes, *Words of Stone*

🍁 WORD ORIGIN *Exasperation* comes from Latin *exasperātiō*, "exasperation." *Exasperātiō* itself comes from the Latin verb *exasperāre*, "to make rough or sore, irritate, exasperate." Latin *exasperāre* is made up of the prefix *ex-* and the Latin verb *asperāre*. The Latin prefix *ex-* literally means "out," but it was also used in Latin to intensify or add a notion of completeness to the meaning of verbs. (The English word *out* can be used in the same way, as in *It worked out well* and *I got tired out,* and in slang expressions like *to veg out,* "to become completely relaxed.") The Latin verb *asperāre* means "to make rough" and comes from the Latin adjective *asper,* "rough." *Asper* is also the source of the English word *asperity* that means "roughness" and "ill temper."

32 exhilarate (ĭg-zĭl'ə-rāt')

verb

To cause someone to feel very happy; elate.

Liyana felt **exhilarated** by the skyscrapers. Their glittering lines lifted her out of her worry. She wished she could ride every sleek elevator up and down, punching buttons, seeing who got on and off. Some days you remembered the world was full of wonderful people you hadn't met yet.

—Naomi Shihab Nye, *Habibi*

WORD ORIGIN *Exhilarate* comes from the Latin verb *exhilalāre,* "to make cheerful." Latin *exhilalāre* comes from the adjective *hilarus,* "cheerful." The English adjective *hilarious* also comes from Latin *hilarus*—a joke that is hilarious makes people feel cheerful.

33 falter (fôl′tər)

verb

To proceed or continue in an unsteady or weakening manner.

> The winding key was still revolving, but more and more slowly. The melody **faltered**. Another few widely spaced notes plinked, and then it stopped.
>
> —Natalie Babbitt, *Tuck Everlasting*

WORD ORIGIN The origin of the English word *falter* is uncertain. It first appears in English in the 1300s. It may be related to Old Norse *faltrask*, "to be puzzled, hesitate." According to another theory, it may come from *fald*, the old form of the verb now spelled *fold* in Modern English. *Fold*, of course, can mean not only "to bend over" but also "to give way, be unable to resist, fail" (as in sentences like *That business folded*). In this way, a horse that falters or stumbles may originally have been one whose legs momentarily fold or give way.

noun

The ability to imagine what is likely to happen in the future.

> Maniac knew what the rest of them didn't: the hardest part was yet to come. He had to find the right routes to untangle the mess, or it would just close up again like a rock and probably stay that way forever. He would need the touch of a surgeon, the alertness of an owl, the cunning of three foxes, and the **foresight** of a grand master in chess.
>
> —Jerry Spinelli, *Maniac Magee*

WORD ORIGIN *Foresight* is made up of the prefix *fore-*, meaning "before, at the front," and *sight*. *Fore-* can be found in many other words relating to the idea of "being in front or before," such as *foreman, forewoman,* and *foretell.* This prefix comes from Old English *fore,* "in front." The prefix usually spelled *for-*, found in such words as *forget* and *forgive,* has a different origin, however. It comes from the Old English *for-* meaning "completely" and also "excessively, to destructive or harmful effect."

35 fragrance (frā′grəns)

noun

A sweet or pleasant odor; a scent.

> He was not hungry. But when Kino begged him he took up his porcelain spoon and drank a little of the soup. It was hot and good, and he smelled its **fragrance** in his nostrils.
> —Pearl S. Buck, *The Big Wave*

WORD ORIGIN *Fragrance* comes from Latin *frāgrantia,* "fragrance." *Frāgrantia* itself comes from Latin *frāgrāre,* "to be fragrant." The present participle of Latin *frāgrāre* was *frāgrāns,* "being fragrant," and *frāgrāns* is the source of the English adjective *fragrant.*

36 furtive (fûr′tĭv)

adjective

1. Done or acting in a way that is intended not to be noticed; sneaky. **2.** Giving the appearance of not wanting to be noticed, especially in showing nervousness.

> He never forgot the hawk, and its moving shadow always sent him crouching into the nearest thicket. He no longer sprawled and straddled, and already he was developing the gait of his mother, slinking and **furtive**, apparently without exertion, yet sliding along with a swiftness that was as deceptive as it was imperceptible.
>
> —Jack London, *White Fang*

> When he reached the crest I saw the ragged uncouth figure outlined for an instant against the cold blue sky. He looked round him with a **furtive** and stealthy air, as one who dreads pursuit. Then he vanished over the hill.
>
> —Sir Arthur Conan Doyle, *The Hound of the Baskervilles*

WORD ORIGIN *Furtive* comes from the Latin word *furtīvus*, which can mean both "obtained by theft" and "stealthy." *Furtīvus* is related to the Latin words *furtum*, "theft," and *fur*, "thief." A person who rummages in a desk drawer furtively searches it like a thief trying to steal something without being noticed.

37 grueling (grōoʹə-lĭng)

adjective

Physically or mentally exhausting.

> Machines ran around the clock, and workers were forced to keep up. A typical working day was fourteen hours long. Men, women, and children kept up this **grueling** schedule six days a week, year after year after year. The result was broken bodies, broken spirits, and broken lives.
>
> —Ruth Ashby, *Victorian England*

WORD ORIGIN The noun *gruel*, of course, usually means simply "porridge," but what exactly is *gruel* doing in *grueling*? In the 1700s, there were several popular expressions using the noun *gruel* to mean "punishment," since lumpy, bland porridge is hard to swallow with any pleasure, and gruel was often fed to prisoners. *To give a man his gruel* meant "to punish a man" or even "to kill a man." Similarly, expressions like *We must take our gruel* meant "We must accept our punishment." In this way, a *grueling experience* is a "punishing experience"—one that feels like a punishment.

38 gusto (gŭs′tō)

noun

Great enjoyment; zest.

> In December 1774, Benedict was one of sixty to join the newly formed militia company in New Haven; in March of the following year he was elected captain. He was thirty-four years old but he took command with the same **gusto** as if he'd been fifteen.
>
> —Jean Fritz, *Traitor: The Case of Benedict Arnold*

WORD ORIGIN *Gusto* comes from Italian *gusto,* meaning "taste," "zest," and "refinement." It entered English in the early 1600s, a period when Italy had a great deal of influence on people's tastes in music, poetry, painting, and even table manners in all parts of Europe—even the use of the fork at the dinner table, for example, spread from Italy to the rest of Europe at this time. The Italian word *gusto* comes from Latin *gustus,* "taste." Latin *gustus* is also the source of the Spanish word *gusto,* "taste," and of English words like *gustatory,* "relating to the sense of taste."

39 habitation (hăb′ĭ-tā′shən)

noun

A place in which to live; a residence.

Late in the evening, tired and happy and miles from home, they drew up on a remote common far from **habitations**, turned the horse loose to graze, and ate their simple supper sitting on the grass by the side of the cart.

—Kenneth Grahame, *The Wind in the Willows*

WORD ORIGIN *Habitation* comes from Latin *habitātiō*, "dwelling, habitation." *Habitātiō* comes from the Latin verb *habitāre*, "to dwell." *Habitāre* is also the source of other English words such as *habitat*, "place where a plant or animal lives," and *inhabitable*, "able to be lived in."

40 hasten (hā′sən)

verb

1. To move or act swiftly; hurry. **2.** To cause something to happen more quickly than it would otherwise.

> He kept close to the buildings, watching out for a policeman who might stop to ask him what he was doing out alone so late. A clock in the window of a jewelry store showed the hour: 11:50. People walked swiftly, as though they were **hastening** home before something happened.
>
> —Paula Fox, *Monkey Island*

> Slaves provided a vast pool of labor that was crucial to the South's war effort. If Lincoln freed the slaves, he could cripple the Confederacy and **hasten** the end of the war. If he did not free them, then the war would settle nothing. Even if the South agreed to return to the Union, it would start another war as soon as slavery was threatened again.
>
> —Russell Freedman, *Lincoln: A Photobiography*

WORD ORIGIN *Hasten* comes from the noun *haste,* meaning "speed" and "overeagerness." *Haste* comes from the Old French word *haste* (now spelled *hâte* in modern French). The French word itself was borrowed from Frankish, the Germanic language of the Franks, a people who conquered France in the 5th century.

41 havoc (hăv′ək)

noun

Very great destruction or disorder.

"Oh, I wouldn't doubt for a minute that you started it, Jane. You cause **havoc** wherever you go. First my poor garden, and now this!" said Mrs. Tifton, indicating the rest of the music room with a dramatic sweep of her arm.

Skye and Jeffrey peered around the grand piano. Oh, no, thought Skye. Maybe there wasn't a spilled urn, but something pretty awful had been added to the music room—a sort of combination Wild West fort and Arabian Nights tent, built from couch pillows and a brass fire screen, plus a dozen large leather-covered books and several elegant silk throws.

—Jeanne Birdsall, *The Penderwicks*

WORD ORIGIN *Havoc* was originally used in the phrase *cry havoc,* "give the signal to soldiers to begin plundering and taking the property of a defeated enemy." In Old French, the shout *Havoc!* or *Havot!* was used as a signal for plundering to begin. The shout is probably borrowed from a Germanic language, and it may be related to the English verb *heave,* "to lift up."

42 **headway** (hĕd′wā′)

noun

Progress toward a destination or a goal.

> In vain she nibbled at the bread and butter and pecked at the crab-apple preserve out of the little scalloped glass dish by her plate. She did not really make any **headway** at all.
> —L. M. Montgomery, *Anne of Green Gables*

🍁 WORD ORIGIN Many everyday words and expressions come from the specialized vocabulary of ships and seafaring used by sailors and fishermen. *Headway,* for example, originated in the 1600s as a nautical term for the progress that a ship made *ahead,* in its set course toward its destination. *Headway* contrasts with *leeway,* a word that originally referred to the distance that a ship had deviated from its set course in the leeward direction—that is, downwind, in the direction toward which the wind is blowing. (Ships deviate from their course in this way because the wind pushes them to the side in the leeward direction.) Nowadays, *leeway* is commonly used with the meaning "a margin of freedom allowed to a person."

He examined the ground closely and found what he had hoped to find—the print of hunting boots. They pointed along the cliff in the direction he had been going. Eagerly he hurried along, now slipping on a rotten log or a loose stone, but making **headway**; night was beginning to settle down on the island.

—Richard Connell, *The Most Dangerous Game*

43 ignite (ĭg-nīt′)

verb

1. To cause something to start burning. **2.** To begin to burn; catch fire.

> In the morning, Timothy began making the fire pile down on the beach. He had a plan. We'd always keep a small fire smoldering up by the hut, and if an airplane came near, he'd take a piece of burning wood from our small fire to **ignite** the big one.
>
> —Theodore Taylor, *The Cay*

> I turned on the video camera and shot Sun-jo lighting the stove, or trying to light the stove. It must have taken him fifty strokes to get the cigarette lighter going in the thin air. When it finally **ignited** his thumb was bleeding like he had sliced it open with a knife.
>
> —Roland Smith, *Peak*

> WORD ORIGIN *Ignite* comes from the Latin verb *ignīre*, "to start on fire." *Ignīre* itself comes from the Latin word for "fire," *ignis*. Latin *ignis* is also the source of such English words as *igneous*, "formed by solidification from a molten state," used to describe rocks that have a fiery origin, so to speak. The Latin word *ignis* is related to the Russian word for fire, *ogon'*, and even the name of the Hindu god of fire, *Agni*.

44 illuminate (ĭ-lo͞o′mə-nāt′)

verb

To provide with light or cast light on someone or something.

> The buildings here were all a lovely misty gray, which gave them a dreamlike quality. They seemed to rise directly out of the rock as if they had been grown, not made by human hands. Maybe they weren't as tall as the skyscrapers Gregor knew by name, but they towered high above his head, some at least thirty stories and finished in artful peaks and turrets. Thousands of torches were placed strategically so that a soft, dusky light **illuminated** the entire city.
>
> —Suzanne Collins, *Gregor the Overlander*

WORD ORIGIN *Illuminate* comes from the Latin verb *illūmināre*, "to throw light on, brighten." *Illūmināre* is made up of the Latin prefix *in-*, meaning "in, into, onto," and the Latin verb *lūmināre*, "to light up." (The prefix *in-* becomes *il-* when it is added to a word beginning with an *l* like *lūmināre*.) The verb *lūmināre* comes from *lūmen*, the Latin word for "light." *Lūmen* is also the source of such English words as *luminary*, "one who is brilliant, who shines by personal talent," and another word that is an entry in this book, *luminous*.

45 impending (ĭm-pĕn′dĭng)

adjective

About to occur.

> Throughout the country was the feeling of **impending** evil. It was as if some unknown terror would come out of the deep shadows.
>
> —Marie McSwigan, *Snow Treasure*

WORD ORIGIN *Impending* is the present participle of the verb *impend*, "to be about to happen." *Impend* comes from Latin *impendēre*, "to hang above, hang over." *Impendēre* is made up of the Latin prefix *in-*, "on," added to the Latin verb *pendēre*, "to hang." Something that is impending is like something that is hanging over you and about to fall, so to speak. The Latin verb *pendēre* is also the source of such English words as *pendant*, "something that hangs from something else, such as an ornament on a necklace," and *suspend*, "to cause to hang, cause to stop for a time."

⭐ 46 imperious (ĭm-pîr′ē-əs)

adjective

Arrogant; overbearing; domineering.

> "Stop, you carriers! I want to speak with the children. I know them." Mrs. Sharpe's **imperious** tone brought everyone to a standstill.
>
> —Blue Balliett, *Chasing Vermeer*

🍁 WORD ORIGIN *Imperious* comes from Latin *imperiōsus,* "imperious." Latin *imperiōsus* comes from Latin *imperium,* "authority, dominion, empire." When someone acts in an imperious way, they act as if they had authority or power over others, when in fact they might not have any authority. The English word *empire* is related to *imperious* and comes from Old French *empire.* Old French *empire* comes from Latin *imperium,* "authority, empire." The difference in spelling between the English noun *empire* and its corresponding adjective *imperial* is explained by the fact that the Latin word *imperium* reached English through the French form *empire.* *Imperial,* on the other hand, comes directly from Latin *imperiālis,* "relating to empire, imperial."

verb

To talk rapidly and in a senseless manner; chatter.

> First, Beth Ann. She called today and **jabbered** on for hours about that wonnnnderful Carl Ray. That cabbageheaded ole Carl Ray sent her a dozen red roses!!!
>
> —Sharon Creech, *Absolutely Normal Chaos*

WORD ORIGIN *Jabber* first appears in English in the very late 1400s. Originally it was probably an example of onomatopoeia—the making of a word to imitate a sound, like *buzz* imitating the sound of a fly. *Jabber* imitates the sound of chattering. Middle English also had several very similar-sounding words with meanings related to *jabber,* such as the verbs *javelen* and *chavelen,* "to chatter."

48 jargon (jär′gən)

noun

The specialized language of a trade, profession, or group of people.

What about me? Barbara began to wonder. What had Rosemary told Greg about his future sister-in-law? She rummaged through Rosemary's secondhand psychology **jargon** for phrases that might fit. Something like, "Barbara's all right but she's terribly immature." Or, "Barbara's all right but she can't get along with Gordy. Sibling rivalry, you know. She feels insecure."

—Beverly Cleary, *Sister of the Bride*

Lura discussed the horse world—important things, like the difference between a Thoroughbred and a purebred; and that Arabians have one less vertebra than other horses, which accounts for their short backs; and the special **jargon** of horse markings, such as stars and stripes, and stockings and socks.

—Marguerite Henry, *Mustang, Wild Spirit of the West*

WORD ORIGIN *Jargon* comes from Middle English *jargon*, which originally meant "the twittering of birds" and also "gibberish." The Middle English word is a borrowing of Old French *jargon*, which could describe not only the twittering of birds but also the specialized slang or lingo used by criminals. Old French *jargon* is related to other French words connected with the throat such as *gargoter*, "to eat messily," and *gargouiller*, "to gargle." (French *gargouiller*, in fact, is the source of the English verb *gargle*.) The elements *garg-* and *jarg-* in these words are examples of what is called *onomatopoeia* because they imitate sounds that are made deep in the throat, like gargling.

⭐ 49 jostle (jŏs′əl)

verb

To bump roughly against another person or thing.

> Tree-ear entered the city gates and stopped in midstep. How crowded it was! People, oxen, and carts **jostled** one another in the narrow streets; the houses were so close together that Tree-ear wondered how their residents could breathe.
>
> —Linda Sue Park, *A Single Shard*

🍁 WORD ORIGIN Many English verbs that refer to repeated, continuing, or forceful actions end in the letters *-le*, like *dribble* and *gobble*. These verbs with the ending *-le* are called *frequentatives* by linguists, since they describe *frequent,* or repeated, actions.

Most frequentative verbs are formed from similar-sounding, related verbs. For example, *sparkle* is the frequentative of the verb *spark,* and *dribble* is the frequentative of the verb *drip.* Sometimes it takes a bit more thought to find the original verb from which a frequentative verb was made. *Dazzle,* for example, began as the frequentative of *daze,* "to stun," while *waddle*, "to walk clumsily," originated as the frequentative of *wade*, "to walk heavily, as through water."

In some cases, frequentative verbs have come to mean something rather different from the original verbs from which they were made—as in the case of *jostle*. *Jostle*, meaning "to bump roughly against another person or thing," was originally the frequentative of the verb *joust*, "to fight with lances on horseback."

50 jut (jŭt)

verb

To extend sharply outward or upward; project.

Hair grew all over Phan Ku. Horns curved up out of his head, and tusks **jutted** from his jaw. In one hand he held a chisel; and with it he carved out the world.

—Virginia Hamilton, *In the Beginning: Creation Stories from Around the World*

WORD ORIGIN The verb *jut* comes from a Middle English noun that was spelled in many different ways, such as *gete* or *iutei,* and meant "a part that sticks out, such as the projecting upper story of a building" and "jetty (a structure that is built out into a body of water)." This Middle English noun survives today in Modern English as the word *jetty.* The Middle English noun came from the Old French word *jetee,* which was a form of the past participle of the verb *jeter,* "to project, throw, spout forth." Old French *jeter* is also the source of the English word *jet,* meaning "a high-speed stream of fluid" and "an airplane propelled by a high-speed stream of fuel."

She led Anson past the farmyard and up an ascent that rose so quickly that soon they were hand in hand, helping each other clamber over the mossy boulders that **jutted** out unexpectedly.

—Gary D. Schmidt, *Anson's Way*

51 kindle (kĭn′dl)

verb

1. To build and start a fire. **2.** To arouse or excite a feeling.

The pioneers had been up since four that morning, when the sentries started the day by firing their rifles. Hurrying about in the darkness, they had **kindled** fires, put on kettles of water, milked cows, pulled down tents, loaded wagons, and fixed breakfast.

—Russell Freedman, *Children of the Wild West*

Anne had certain rose-tinted ideals of what a teacher might accomplish if she only went the right way about it; and she was in the midst of a delightful scene, forty years hence, with a famous personage . . . just exactly what he was to be famous for was left in convenient haziness, but Anne thought it would be rather nice to have him a college president or a Canadian premier . . . bowing low over her wrinkled hand and assuring her that it was she who had first **kindled** his ambition, and that all his success in life was due to the lessons she had instilled so long ago in Avonlea school.

—L. M. Montgomery, *Anne of Avonlea*

WORD ORIGIN *Kindle* comes from Middle English *kindelen,* "to kindle." *Kindelen* is probably a borrowing of Old Norse *kynda,* "to kindle."

52 knoll (nōl)

noun

A small, rounded hill.

When the Sillingtons first settled in Clarion County, before there was a state road parallel to the lake, they owned all the land down to the water's edge. The house itself is perched atop a **knoll**, and from the upstairs windows you get a good view of the lake.

—E. L. Konigsburg, *The View from Saturday*

WORD ORIGIN *Knoll* comes from the Middle English world *knoll*, and Middle English *knoll* comes from Old English *cnoll*, "little hill, knoll." *Knoll* is related to words in other members of the Germanic language group, such as Dutch *knol*, "lump, clod," and German *Knoll*, "lump, bulb." In Dutch and German, the *k* at the beginning of such words is pronounced just like any other *k*, so these words begin with a consonant cluster that sounds a little odd to people who speak English. But in earlier times, English speakers pronounced the *k*'s in words beginning with the letters *kn*, like *knee* and *know*. In the 1600s, the *k* stopped being pronounced, but the spelling of the words was not changed to reflect the change in pronunciation.

53 luminous (lōō′mə-nəs)

adjective

Giving off light; shining.

It was almost exactly two hours later that Jessica found herself suddenly wide awake and staring through the darkness at the **luminous** hands of her clock.

—Zilpha Keatley Snyder, *The Witches of Worm*

WORD ORIGIN The word *luminous* comes from Latin *lūminōsus,* "full of light, luminous." *Lūminōsus* itself comes from the Latin word for "light," *lūmen.* *Lūmen* is also the source of another English word that is an entry in this book, *illuminate.*

★ 54 malleable (măl′ē-ə-bəl)

adjective

Capable of being shaped or formed by pressing, hammering, or another forceful action.

> The throne itself was of pure, unalloyed gold, and since pure, unalloyed gold is almost as **malleable** as clay, a crew of dragon goldsmiths was kept busy all the time repairing the throne where the Lord might have dented it.
>
> —Laurence Yep, *Dragonwings*

WORD ORIGIN *Malleable* comes from Latin *malleābilis,* "able to be hammered into shape, malleable." *Malleābilis* comes from the Latin verb *malleāre,* "to hammer," which itself comes from Latin *malleus,* "hammer." Other English words that come from *malleus* are *mallet,* "a short-handled hammer with a large head," and *maul,* "a large, long-handled hammer used to pound stakes."

⭐ 55 materialize (mə-tîr′ē-ə-līz′)

verb

To appear out of nowhere.

> Although pests like mice, cockroaches, and mosquitoes sometimes seem to **materialize** out of thin air, by the 18th century just about everyone agreed that they were born from parents of the same species, not from muck or swamp water.
>
> —Louise E. Robbins, *Louis Pasteur and the Hidden World of Microbes*

🍁 WORD ORIGIN The verb *materialize* was made by adding the suffix *-ize* (which makes verbs out of nouns and adjectives) to the word *material* (which is both a noun meaning "substance" and an adjective meaning "made of matter"). *Material* comes from the Latin noun *māteria*, "matter." Latin *māteria* is also the source of the English word *matter*.

⭐ 56 meander (mē-ăn′dər)

verb

To follow a winding and turning course.

> Snug in their furs, the two children ran out across the great snow-covered slope in front of the house, through the grove, and down to where a frozen river **meandered** across the park, after falling over two or three artificial cascades, now stiff and gleaming with icicles.
>
> —Joan Aiken, *The Wolves of Willoughby Chase*

🍁 WORD ORIGIN The word *meander* comes from the ancient Greek name of a river in Turkey. In Turkish, the river is now called the *Büyük Menderes*. It rises in west central Turkey and flows westward along a course with many very small windings before it finally empties into the Aegean Sea. The ancient Greeks called the river the *Maiandros*, and it was famous among them for its tortuous, winding course. The Greeks compared anything that had a winding appearance, such as a decorative pattern, to the Maiandros. The Romans borrowed the name of the river from the Greeks and used it as a noun, *maeander*, to mean "a winding course, a wavy line." Eventually the Latin word came into English as *meander*.

"Lettuce," she announced later, pulling a head out of the plastic bag in front of us, "should be leafy, not slimy. And no black or brown edges. . . . A bad piece of lettuce can ruin your whole day."

"Right," I said.

"Chop it like this," she instructed, taking a few whacks with a knife before handing it to me. "Big chops, but not too big."

I chopped. She watched. "Good," she said, reaching over to adjust my chops just a bit. I went on. "Very good."

Morgan was this **meticulous** about everything.

—Sarah Dessen, *Keeping the Moon*

57 meticulous (mĭ-tĭk′yə-ləs)

adjective

Showing great concern for details; extremely careful or precise.

> The judge waited for the doorman to enter the information in his slow, cramped lettering. He had to be **meticulous** in order to prove he was better than his eighth-grade education. It's a pity he had not gone further, he was quite a clever man.
>
> —Ellen Raskin, *The Westing Game*

> Because it was too cold and snowy to go to school, Ma made Mary and Laura do some schoolwork, and she also started both Mary and Laura on making a simple nine-square quilt. Mary loved the **meticulous** work of piecing the bits of used cloth together so that the fabric had no puckers and the stitches were perfectly straight and even, but Laura found every stitch a chore.
>
> —Janet & Geoff Benge, *Laura Ingalls Wilder: A Storybook Life*

WORD ORIGIN The English word *meticulous* originally meant "fearful." Because a person who is fearful of making a mistake will take great care while performing a task, *meticulous* came to mean "extremely careful." *Meticulous* comes from the Latin word *metĭculōsus*, "fearful." *Metĭculōsus* itself comes from the Latin word for "fear," *metus*. English doesn't have many other words that come from Latin *metus*, but *metus* is the source of the usual word for "fear" in Spanish, *miedo*.

58 misgivings (mĭs-gĭv′ĭngs)

plural noun

Feelings of doubt or concern.

By now, the president had serious **misgivings** about the professional soldiers who were running the war. He had collected a library of books on military strategy, and he studied them late into the night, just as he had once studied law and surveying.

—Russell Freedman, *Lincoln: A Photobiography*

🍁 WORD ORIGIN In origin, the word *misgivings* comes from the gerund of the archaic verb *misgive,* "to cause a person doubt or concern." (A gerund is the noun form of a verb made by adding the ending -*ing.*) The verb *misgive* is a compound made up of the prefix *mis-* and the verb *give. Mis-* means "badly" or "wrongly" (as in *mistake* or *misguided*), while the common verb *give* also used to have the meaning "suggest."

Misgive was used in such sentences as *My heart misgave me* or *My mind misgave me.* Literally, these sentences mean "My heart (or mind) caused me feelings of concern," but we would probably express the same idea in Modern English as *I felt concern* or *I had misgivings.* Although *misgive* is rarely used as a verb in Modern English, the gerund of *misgive* is still in common use as *misgivings,* "feelings of concern."

⭐59 momentum (mō-mĕn′təm)

noun

A quantity used to measure the motion of a body, equal to the product of its mass and velocity. Any change in the speed or direction of a body changes its momentum.

> Ralph discovered that if he made the noise fast, the motorcycle speeded up. If he slowed the sound, the motorcycle slowed down. He promptly speeded up and raced around in the rectangle of moonlight, where he made another discovery. When he ran out of breath, the **momentum** of the motorcycle carried him on until he could take another breath.
>
> —Beverly Cleary, *The Mouse and the Motorcycle*

WORD ORIGIN In the 1600s and 1700s, scientists like Galileo Galilei, René Descartes, and Isaac Newton tried to develop a complete theory of how forces act on objects. They needed a word for the quantity equal to the mass of a body in motion times its velocity. Eventually the Latin noun *mōmentum*, "movement," was chosen as a name for this quantity, and this word began to be used in English as *momentum*. The Latin noun *mōmentum* comes from the verb *movēre*, "to move," also the source of another English word that is an entry in this book, *commotion*.

⭐ 60 monotonous (mə-nŏt′n-əs)

adjective

Dull because of being always the same.

No matter how carefully each family planned and packed, however, the Emigrant Trail was potholed with unforeseen troubles. Accidents could set a family back a day or more for repairs or doctoring; at worst, an accident could mean sudden death. A child falling from a wagon could be crushed by wagon wheels in a heartbeat. A storm-swollen river might sweep a whole wagon away during a crossing. Lightning-strikes or hailstorms could extinguish a life on an otherwise dull and **monotonous** day.

—Linda Crew, *A Heart for Any Fate*

WORD ORIGIN *Monotonous* comes from Greek *monotonos*, "monotonous." Greek *monotonos* is a compound made from the word *monos*, "single," and *tonos*, "pitch, key, or musical scale in which a piece of music is composed." Greek *monos* is also the source of many English words relating to the idea of "one" or "single," such as *monochromatic*, "painted or drawn using one color," and *monopoly*, "the production and control of a product by a single company." Greek *tonos* is the source of the English word *tone*.

Clicketta, clicketta, clicketta. The song of the locomotive was **monotonous** as they traveled north, and the hours seemed like Mama's never-ending ball of thread unwinding in front of them.

—Pam Muñoz Ryan, *Esperanza Rising*

61 multitude (mŭl′tĭ-tōōd′)

noun

A very large number.

> Though it was only May it was as hot as the hot height of summer. The fields with their **multitude** of restless insects stretched far and wide.
>
> —Eleanor Estes, *Ginger Pye*

WORD ORIGIN *Multitude* comes from Latin *multitūdō*, "multitude." *Multitūdō* comes from *multus*, "many." Latin *multus* is also the source of the prefix *multi-* that can be found in many other English words relating to the notion of "being many." These include *multifaceted*, "having many facets," *multimillionaire*, "a person having several million dollars," and *multiply*, "to make or become numerous."

---

62 muster (mŭs′tər)

verb

1. To bring a group of soldiers together; assemble. **2.** To bring forth a feeling or ability from within oneself.

Past Trinity Chapel, its bronze bells still so new as not to have entirely greened, and on to New Barracks at last. Here everything was familiar. The red coats of the Staffordshire Fencibles blended with the red coats of Fifeshire Fencibles, Yorkshire Foot Guards, and Herefordshire Light Dragoons. The colonel **mustered** the Fencibles on the quadrangle before the barracks, eyeing them for the slightest misstep and pushing up an eyebrow when he saw one.

—Gary D. Schmidt, *Anson's Way*

Alfonso walked with the girl and the boy as they started for home. They didn't talk much. Every few steps, the girl, whose name was Sandra, would look at him out of the corner of her eye, and Alfonso would look away. He learned that she was in seventh grade, just like him, and that she had a pet terrier named Queenie. Her father was a mechanic at Rudy's Speedy Repair, and her mother was a teacher's aide at Jefferson Elementary.

When they came to the street, Alfonso and Sandra stopped at her corner, but her brother ran home. Alfonso watched him stop in the front yard to talk to a lady he guessed was their mother. She was raking leaves into a pile.

"I live over there," she said, pointing.

Alfonso looked over her shoulder for a long time, trying to **muster** enough nerve to ask her if she'd like to go bike riding tomorrow.

—Gary Soto, "Broken Chain," *Baseball in April and Other Stories*

WORD ORIGIN *Muster* comes from Old French *moustrer*, "to muster troops for inspection." Old French *moustrer* comes from the Latin verb *mōnstrāre*, "to show," and *mōnstrāre* comes from the Latin noun *mōnstrum*, which basically meant "an unnatural thing or event regarded as a sign from the gods." The Romans believed that when the gods were displeased, they showed their anger by causing animals to give birth to deformed young. In this way, *mōnstrum* came to mean not only "unnatural thing regarded as a sign" but also "horrible-looking creature." Other English words that come from *mōnstrum*, "horrible-looking creature," are *monster* and *monstrosity*.

63 narrate (năr′āt′)

verb

1. To tell a story or describe a series of events.
2. To provide or read the spoken comments for a documentary or other video.

> Sara not only could tell stories, but she adored telling them. When she sat or stood in the midst of a circle and began to invent wonderful things, her green eyes grew big and shining, her cheeks flushed, and, without knowing that she was doing it, she began to act and made what she told lovely or alarming by the raising or dropping of her voice, the bend and sway of her slim body, and the dramatic movement of her hands. She forgot that she was talking to listening children; she saw and lived with the fairy folk, or the kings and queens and beautiful ladies, whose adventures she was **narrating**.
>
> —Frances Hodgson Burnett, *A Little Princess*

Woody met a film director who was planning to make a documentary movie about the Grand Coulee Dam on the Columbia River in Oregon. The director needed someone to **narrate** the film, and he interviewed Woody for the part. In early May 1941, desperate and not yet knowing if he would be hired, Woody loaded the family into the car and headed for Portland, Oregon.

—Karen Mueller Coombs, *Woody Guthrie: America's Folksinger*

WORD ORIGIN *Narrate* comes from the Latin verb *narrāre*, meaning "to tell, describe, narrate." *Narrāre* is related to the Latin adjective *gnārus*, "knowing, expert." Someone who knows a story can retell it to others.

The Latin word *gnārus*, "knowing," is in fact distantly related to the English word *know*. *Know* is a native English word (that is, a word that came down directly from the Germanic ancestor of Old English, rather than being borrowed from another language like French or Latin). Linguists think that Latin and the Germanic languages developed from a language that was spoken thousands of years ago. Many other languages of Asia and Europe—including Hindi, Persian, Greek, the Slavic languages like Russian and Polish, and the Celtic languages like Irish and Welsh—also developed from this pre-historic ancestor language. We can tell this from similar patterns in the words. Wherever Latin has a word beginning with *g*, like *gnārus*, "knowing," the related native English word will usually begin with a *k* or *c*, like *know*. Other examples include Latin *genū*, "knee," and English *knee*, and Latin *gelū*, "frost," and English *cold*.

64 obscure (əb-skyŏŏr′)

adjective

1. Difficult to understand; vague. **2.** Not widely known about.

verb

To conceal from view; hide.

> I turn the paper on its head, and see that I am mistaken. It was not written by a Shao Lin monk. It is, in fact, a musical composition. I vaguely recognize several **obscure** musical symbols, and there are also several dozen notes that seem to be jumping about the page like fleas on a dog, playing hide-and-seek amid the musical bars.
>
> —David Klass, *You Don't Know Me*

> It would be nice to say the year ends on this note, that we walk away feeling bigger and better because we set a goal and met it, that a bunch of **obscure** guys who never had friends before, now have friends and life looks different. And that's all true, but that isn't how it ends.
>
> —Chris Crutcher, *Whale Talk*

She came to within three yards of Sally and stopped. The ancient crooked bonnet she wore **obscured** the top part of her face so that only her mouth and chin could be seen clearly, her mouth working all the time as if she were chewing something small and resistant; but still the eyes glittered in the darkness.

—Philip Pullman, *The Ruby in the Smoke*

WORD ORIGIN *Obscure* comes from Latin *obscūrus*, "dark." The origin of the Latin word *obscūrus* itself is a little obscure, however. The word looks like a compound of the Latin prefix *ob*, "against," and the word-element *-scūrus*. This element *-scūrus* may come from a word root *skū*, which is the source of words relating to the notion of "covering" or "concealing" in many languages related to Latin. The English word *sky*, for example, comes from the Old Norse word *skȳ*, "cloud," and Old Norse *skȳ* comes from the root *skū-*. (A cloud is something that covers the blue heavens above it, so to speak.) In origin, therefore, *obscūrus* meant something like "covered or concealed against being seen."

65 ominous (ŏm′ə-nəs)

adjective

Being a sign of trouble, danger, or disaster; threatening.

> The sun was above the bamboo trees now, and carrying his heavy bundle made him hotter. He hurried to Shoichi's house, meeting no one on the street and feeling the silence **ominous**.
>
> —Yoko Kawashima Watkins, *So Far from the Bamboo Grove*

WORD ORIGIN Like many ancient peoples, the Romans believed that they could predict large, important events by observing other, seemingly unrelated events, such as how a bird flew off in a particular direction. The Romans would also sacrifice animals and look for signs of things to come in the look and shape of the sacrificed animal's organs. The Latin word for the signs that the Romans thought they saw was *ōmen*—the source of our word *omen*, "a prophetic sign." An *ōmen* could also be a larger event, such as the appearance of a comet. Before beginning any big project, the ancient Romans looked for omens to find out if the gods were favorable to the project. Something that seemed to predict an unfavorable outcome was called *ōminōsus*, "ominous," and *ōminōsus* is the source of our word *ominous*.

Not everyone had an easy crossing. Many slipped on the treacherous ice or were blown over by the still-fierce wind. A few of the elderly adventurers had to be carried to shore. For over an hour and a half, people and animals paraded from one shore to the other. While no one kept an official count, the policemen on duty that day estimated that between 1,500 and 3,000 walked across the river.

The cheerful mood of the crowd began to subside just after 9 A.M. That was when a deep, **ominous** grumbling began coming from the ice. The tide was beginning to shift, pushing at the ice to shove it downriver.

—Jim Murphy, *Blizzard!*

66 outlandish (out-lăn′dĭsh)

adjective

Unconventional; strange.

> Likely they had never seen a girl *not* decked out in silk and damask, *not* bathed and scrubbed raw, *not* brushed and perfumed until she gleamed and reeked of flowers. They looked at me as if I were some **outlandish** creature.
>
> —Susan Fletcher, *Shadow Spinner*

> Coming to this fortress are warriors of every kind, from every world. Men and women, yes, and fighting spirits, too, and armed creatures such as I had never seen—lizards and apes, great birds with poison spurs, creatures too **outlandish** to have a name I could guess at.
>
> —Philip Pullman, *The Subtle Knife*

WORD ORIGIN *Outlandish* has been around a long time in English. The Old English spelling of the word was *ūtlendisc*. The sound (sh) was spelled *sc* in Old English times, so the Old English suffix *-isc* was not pronounced very much differently from its Modern English descendant, *-ish*. In Old English, *ūtland*, literally "out-land," meant "foreign country."

The *ūt* in this word is the Old English word that became Modern English *out*, and the *land* is the Old English word that became Modern English *land*.

The adjective *ūtlendisc*, "foreign," was made from *ūtland* by adding the Old English suffix *-isc* and changing the vowel in the word *land*. Eventually, Old English *ūtlendisc* developed into Middle English *outlandish*, "foreign." However, the customs of foreigners and items imported from foreign countries can seem strange, and in the 1500s, *outlandish* began to acquire the meaning that it has most often in Modern English, "unconventional, strange."

Crying is all right in its way while it lasts. But you have to stop sooner or later, and then you still have to decide what to do. When Jill stopped, she found she was dreadfully thirsty. She had been lying face downward, and now she sat up. The birds had ceased singing and there was perfect silence except for one small, **persistent** sound, which seemed to come from a good distance away. She listened carefully, and felt almost sure it was the sound of running water.

—C. S. Lewis, *The Silver Chair*

67 persistent (pər-sĭs′tənt)

adjective

1. Refusing to give up or stop; continuing despite difficulties. **2.** Repeating or continuing without stopping.

> Rowdy isn't a fast reader, but he's **persistent**. And he'll just laugh and laugh at the dumb jokes, no matter how many times he's read the same comic.
>
> —Sherman Alexie, *The Absolutely True Diary of a Part-Time Indian*

> He was still by the sink with his back to her, and he could feel her presence like a **persistent** itch. He decided to do the few dishes there were, hoping she'd be gone by the time he finished.
>
> —Kevin Henkes, *Sun & Spoon*

WORD ORIGIN *Persistent* comes from the Latin word *persistēns*, "persisting," which is the present participle of the Latin verb *persistere*, "to persist." *Persistere* is a compound of the Latin prefix *per-* and the Latin verb *sistere*. *Per-*, literally meaning "through" or "thoroughly," is used to strengthen the meanings of verbs, and *sistere* means "to stand, to make stand." Something that is persistent keeps on standing and won't be moved from its purpose, so to speak. Latin *sistere* makes up part of another Latin verb, *exsistere*, "to stand forth, emerge, become visible, exist," which is the source of English *exist. Sistere* can also be found in Latin *insistere*, "to stand on, step upon, dwell on a subject at length," the source of the English verb *insist*.

68 pertinent (pûr′tn-ənt)

adjective

Related to the matter at hand; relevant.

As we followed a few steps behind him, Charlene handed me
some sheets of yellow paper and a thick, eraserless pen-
cil. "You really want to be a reporter, then we'll let this be
your first assignment. Write down everything that you con-
sider **pertinent** to the fact that a prisoner has escaped."

—Bette Greene, *Summer of My German
Soldier*

WORD ORIGIN *Pertinent* is the adjective corresponding to the verb *pertain*. *Pertinent* comes from
the Latin word *pertinēns*, which is the present participle of the Latin verb *pertinēre*, "to reach, extend,
be relevant, pertain."

---

69 potential (pə-tĕn′shəl)

noun

The ability to grow, develop, or improve.

> "You're *alive*, Bod. That means you have infinite **potential**.
> You can do anything, make anything, dream anything. If
> you change the world, the world will change. **Potential**. Once
> you're dead, it's gone. Over. You've made what you've made,
> dreamed your dream, written your name. You may be buried
> here, you may even walk. But that **potential** is finished."
>
> —Neil Gaiman, *The Graveyard Book*

WORD ORIGIN *Potential* comes from the Latin
adjective *potentiālis*, "possible." A person's potential
is what it is possible for him or her to do in the future. The Latin adjective *potentiālis* comes from the
Latin noun *potentia*, "power," and *potentia* comes
from *potēns*, "being able," present participle of the
Latin verb *posse*, "to be able." Latin *potēns* is also the
source of the English word *potent*, "effective, having
a strong effect," and the Latin verb *posse*, "to be able,"
is also the source of the English word *possible*.

70 precipice (prĕs′ə-pĭs)

noun

A very steep or overhanging mass of rock, such as the face of a cliff.

> The eagle came back, seized him in his talons by the back of his coat, and swooped off. This time he flew only a short way. Very soon Bilbo was laid down, trembling with fear, on a wide shelf of rock on the mountain-side. There was no path down onto it save by flying; and no path down off it except by jumping over a **precipice**.
>
> —J. R. R. Tolkien, *The Hobbit*

WORD ORIGIN *Precipice* comes from *praecipitium,* "a fall from a great height." Latin *praecipitium* comes from the Latin adjective *praeceps,* "headlong." The Latin adjective *praeceps* is a compound made up of the Latin prefix *prae-,* "in front, ahead," and the noun *caput,* "head." A precipice is a place where one can take a headlong fall, so to speak. The Latin noun *caput* is also the source of the English word *capital* used to describe the "head city" or center of government of an area.

71 pristine (prĭs′tēn′)

adjective

Remaining in a pure or unspoiled state.

> It turned out that the *Britannic* was in even better shape than I'd dared hope. Yes, she was encrusted with a thin layer of barnacles and coral, but the hull and upper decks were amazingly well preserved. The outer covering that protected the dome over the grand staircase remained intact—most of the panes of glass were still in place! The railings and items of deck hardware looked only in need of a wire brush to return them to an almost **pristine** state.
>
> —Robert D. Ballard, *Ghost Liners*

WORD ORIGIN *Pristine* comes from Latin *pristīnus,* which means "belonging to ancient times" and also "in an original state or condition." It is related to the Latin word *prīmus,* "first"—something that is pristine remains in its original, or first, state. A pristine forest, for example, is one that human beings have not altered by logging and in which all the original species of plants and animals still live.

 **72 quell** (kwĕl)

verb

To cause a feeling to become less intense; calm or settle.

> ". . . The ship is scheduled to leave with the first tide tomor-
> row morning. So there can be *no* delay."
>   To prove the point he turned to move again. I, however,
> unable to **quell** my excited curiosity, managed to slip in one
> more question.
>
> —Avi, *The True Confessions of Charlotte Doyle*

WORD ORIGIN *Quell* comes from the Middle English verb *quellen,* and the Middle English verb comes from the Old English verb *cwellan,* "to kill." To quell people's curiosity is to kill it, so to speak.

She awoke with a start a short time later and looked about in puzzlement. The sky vaulted above her. A grass blade tickled her face, and she remembered where she was—up on the frost heave with the wolf pack! Breathing deeply to **quell** a sense of uneasiness, she finally relaxed, unrolled, and sat up.

—Jean Craighead George, *Julie of the Wolves*

73 recluse (rĕk′lōōs′ *or* rĭ-klōōs′)

noun

A person who lives alone or has little to do with other people.

> Hal was not just a typical introverted artist. Sometime in the last year he had become an actual **recluse**. He didn't come out of his room except, as far as anyone could tell, in the middle of the night, when he was reasonably certain everyone else would be asleep.
>
> —Stephanie S. Tolan, *Surviving the Applewhites*

🍁 WORD ORIGIN *Recluse* comes from the Latin word *reclūsus*, "shut up," the past participle of the verb *reclūdere*, "to shut up." *Reclūdere* is a compound made up of the Latin prefix *re-* and the Latin verb *claudere*, "to close." The prefix *re-* literally means "again" but is also used to strengthen the meaning of verbs. English has many other words that are ultimately derived from the Latin verb *claudere*. These include *seclude*, "to keep apart from contact with others" (from Latin *sēclūdere*, "to close off"), and the verb *include* itself (from Latin *inclūdere*, "to enclose in a sealed receptacle").

★74 recuperate (rĭ-kōō′pə-rāt′)

verb

To return to normal health or strength; recover.

> We hadn't walked far before Grandfather shook with chills....
>
> I bit the inside of my cheek to force back the tears. Crying wouldn't help anything. I put my hand on Grandfather's forehead. It was hot and dripping.
>
> Think, I commanded myself. We have no food or water. We're at least ten miles out of the city. It would take hours to walk back, even if Grandfather felt well....
>
> ...With fresh water and food, we could stay under the willow until he regained his strength, then head back to the city. Grandfather would **recuperate** at home with Mother, and I could care for them both.
>
> —Laurie Halse Anderson, *Fever 1793*

🍁 W O R D   O R I G I N   *Recuperate* comes from the Latin verb *recuperāre,* "to get back, regain." *Recuperāre* is a compound made up of the Latin prefix *re-*, "back, again," and the Latin verb *capere,* "to take." To recuperate is to regain one's strength.

75 replenish (rĭ-plĕn′ĭsh)

verb

To build up a supply of something again; fill again.

> The moon was full when the boys left, and full a month later when Old Tallow returned with her dogs. Many things happened in that time. The women made a new camp. They **replenished** their store of dried meat. They fished and trapped. They found a rice bay and busied themselves harvesting every grain.
>
> —Louise Erdrich, *The Porcupine Year*

WORD ORIGIN *Replenish* comes from the Old French verb *replenir,* "to replenish." *Replenir* is a compound of the Old French prefix *re-,* "back to an original state, again," and the Old French verb *plenir,* "to fill." The verb *plenir* comes from Old French *plein,* "full." Old French *plein,* "full," is also the source of the Old French word *plenté,* "abundance," the source of the English word *plenty.*

⭐ 76 repugnant (rĭ-pŭg′nənt)

adjective

Causing disgust; offensive or repulsive.

> "You have no cause to be alarmed, Captain. My father, though some of his ventures were undoubtedly illegal, was . . . is . . . a noble man. The idea of harming another creature would be **repugnant** to him."
>
> —Eoin Colfer, *Artemis Fowl: The Arctic Incident*

🍁 WORD ORIGIN The original meanings of *repugnant* in English were "hostile" and "contradicting something." In the 1700s, *repugnant* began to be used in the modern sense of "repulsive." *Repugnant* comes from the Latin word *repugnāns*, "fighting back," the present participle of *repugnāre*, "to offer resistance, fight back." *Repugnāre* is a compound of the Latin prefix *re-*, "back," and the Latin verb *pugnāre*, "to fight." *Pugnāre* is also the source of the Latin adjective *pugnāx*, "eager to fight," which is the source of the English word *pugnacious*, "ready or eager to fight."

77 restitution (rĕs′tĭ-tōō′shən)

noun

The act of doing something or paying money to make up for some damage, loss, or injury that you have caused.

When we got home that night, my father phoned the carpenters and the plasterers. He told them that he didn't care that it was late on a Friday night. And he didn't care that tomorrow was a Saturday. They had better be at the house first thing in the morning, ready to fix the ceiling permanently and to offer **restitution** for the property damage their carelessness had caused.

—Gary D. Schmidt, *The Wednesday Wars*

WORD ORIGIN *Restitution* comes from Latin *restitūtiō*, meaning "the act of setting up again, restoring, restitution." *Restitūtiō* comes from the Latin verb *restituere,* "to set up again, put back in place." *Restituere* is a compound of the Latin prefix *re-,* "back, again," and the Latin verb *statuere,* "to set up." The English word *statue* also comes from *statuere.* A statue is "something that is set up" (as a public monument, for example).

sabotage (săb′ə-täzh′)

noun

A deliberate and usually secret act that causes damage or hinders an activity.

verb

To commit sabotage against something.

"So you left the train and it derailed a few moments later?"

She didn't need to add: "That's some coincidence." It was in her eyes and the tone of her voice.

"Well, yes, not just moments later. It was a few minutes after I'd got off."

"It must have been very close if the soldiers from the train chased you and caught you."

"I guess it was close, but not that close."

I was embarrassed by such a lame answer.

"What made the train derail?"

"I don't know. Maybe it was an accident, maybe it was **sabotage**."

—John Marsden, *The Other Side of Dawn*

I had no idea what Dr. Willner had said to Coach Pete, or what the coach had riding on this. It showed what a good guy Coach Pete was that he'd said nothing about it, one way or the other. He hadn't told us to lose or to make Pleasant Valley feel better, even though his job—and for all I knew, his life—might be depending on it. He'd done the legal, acceptable limit of what could be done to **sabotage** the game. He'd let the second string start and play the whole time. But even that hadn't been enough.

—Francine Prose, *After*

WORD ORIGIN In the past, leather shoes were expensive. Many people wore shoes carved out of a single piece of wood. The French word for this kind of shoe is *sabot*. The French created the word *sabotage*, meaning "ruining something by doing a clumsy job," from the word *sabot*, since wooden shoes can be heavy and noisy. The word also came to mean "ruining equipment deliberately," and later, English borrowed the word *sabotage*.

⭐ 79 scarcity (skâr′sĭ-tē)

noun

An insufficient amount or supply; a shortage.

> Because of the **scarcity** of water, each camper was only allowed a four-minute shower. It took Stanley nearly that long to get used to the cold water. There was no knob for hot water. He kept stepping into, then jumping back from, the spray, until the water turned off automatically. He never managed to use his bar of soap, which was just as well, because he wouldn't have had time to rinse off the suds.
>
> —Louis Sachar, *Holes*

🍁 WORD ORIGIN *Scarcity* is the noun, made with the noun-forming suffix *-ity*, corresponding to the adjective *scarce*. *Scarce* itself comes from an Old French word spelled both *escars* and *scars*, "stingy, scanty, scarce."

★80 scurry (skûr′ē)

verb

To move with light running steps; scamper.

As they turned to enter their building, both girls looked straight ahead, toward the door. They did it purposely so that they would not catch the eyes or the attention of two more soldiers, who stood with their guns on this corner as well. Kirsti **scurried** ahead of them through the door, chattering about the picture she was bringing home from kindergarten to show Mama. For Kirsti, the soldiers were simply part of the landscape, something that had always been there, on every corner, as unimportant as lampposts, throughout her remembered life.

—Lois Lowry, *Number the Stars*

🍁 W O R D   O R I G I N *Scurry* is probably short for an earlier expression *hurry-scurry,* "in a confused hurry, helter-skelter." *Hurry-scurry* itself is made of the common verb *hurry,* "to move in haste," and an old-fashioned verb *scurry,* "to go out as a military scout, go out to scout out an area," no longer used in Modern English. This old verb *scurry* was created by subtracting the suffix *-er* from the noun *scurrier,* an old-fashioned term for a military scout, especially one on horseback. *Scurrier* is a shortened form of the Old French word *descouvreor,* literally "discoverer," from the Old French verb *descouvrir,* "to discover." This Old French verb is also the source of English *discover.* In this way, the verb *scurry* , "to scamper," is distantly related to the verb *discover.*

Gaily striped tents and pavilions sprang up everywhere as the workmen **scurried** about like ants. Within minutes there were racecourses and grandstands, side shows and refreshment booths, gaming fields, Ferris wheels, banners, bunting, and bedlam, almost without pause.

—Norton Juster, *The Phantom Tollbooth*

noun

The quality of being calm, peaceful, or untroubled.

Just then Min's wife came around the house with a basket of laundry. Tree-ear jumped to his feet to help her. She nodded her thanks, calm as ever, as if the tumultuous events of the past few days had never happened. They stood on either side of the clothesline; he handed her the garments and she hung them. Her **serenity** and the rhythm of the task helped soothe Tree-ear's raw nerves.

—Linda Sue Park, *A Single Shard*

WORD ORIGIN *Serenity* comes from the Latin noun *serēnitās,* which basically means "a spell of fine weather with clear skies." By extension, *serēnitās* could also mean "favorable circumstances." Latin *serēnitās* comes from the Latin adjective *serēnus,* "clear, cloudless," and "free from trouble." *Serēnus* is the source of the English word *serene.*

Surely her mother must know what people were saying, must be aware of the smugly vicious gossip. Surely it must hurt her as it did Meg. But if it did she gave no outward sign. Nothing ruffled the **serenity** of her expression.

—Madeleine L'Engle, *A Wrinkle in Time*

82 sociable (sō′shə-bəl)

adjective

Enjoying the company of others; friendly.

> After we had been out two or three times together we grew quite friendly and **sociable,** which made me feel very much at home.
>
> —Anna Sewell, *Black Beauty*

WORD ORIGIN *Sociable* comes from the Latin adjective *sociābilis,* "close, intimate," and "easy to join up with." *Sociābilis* comes from the Latin verb *sociāre,* "to share, join," and *sociāre* comes from the Latin noun *socius,* "companion." *Socius* is the source of many other English words relating to the concept of being friendly or getting along with others, such as *social* and *society.*

83 somber (sŏm′bər)

adjective

Very serious or sad.

> She could, in the presence of her cello teacher, Mr. Porch, summon up the most glorious notes; pure, in fact, surprising even Minna. She played beautifully for Mr. Porch, mostly because she wanted to make him smile, as **somber** as he sometimes was.
>
> —Patricia MacLachlan, *The Facts and Fictions of Minna Pratt*

WORD ORIGIN *Somber* is a borrowing of the French word *sombre,* "dark, gloomy." This French word ultimately comes from the Latin phrase *sub umbrā*, "in shadow" (literally, "under a shadow"). *Sub* is the Latin word for "under," and *umbrā* is the form of the Latin noun *umbra*, "shadow," that is used after many prepositions.

84 specimen (spĕs′ə-mən)

noun

Something that is studied by scientists as an example of an entire set of things, such as an entire species of living things.

> Now that she had both feet firmly on the ground, she thought the fossil was well worth the risk she had taken. It was the prize **specimen** of her collection.
> —Cynthia DeFelice, *The Ghost of Fossil Glen*

WORD ORIGIN *Specimen* comes from the Latin noun *specimen*, meaning "a sign, an outward indication of a quality," and also "an example." The Latin word *specimen* itself comes from the Latin verb *specere*, "to look at." Specimens are examples that scientists or technicians look at to determine the properties of a group. Other words coming from Latin *specere* are *perspective*, "a way of seeing things," *spectacle*, "an event worth seeing," and *spectator*, "one who sees an event."

85 stamina (stăm′ə-nə)

noun

The power to resist fatigue or illness while working hard; endurance.

> "There 'e is," screeched Ma, and the chase was on again. They surprised me, Pa especially, with their **stamina**. I had not thought they would last so long. For at least a half-mile they chased me down the uncobbled narrow alleys and the filthy streets, tripping over bodies and avoiding snatching hands, all the way to the river.
>
> —F. E. Higgins, *The Black Book of Secrets*

> Mr. Ellis then led them in a long exercise routine, starting with simple stretching skills and progressing first to slow arm and leg movements and finally to vigorous activities for the entire body. Selina joined in wholeheartedly, determined to qualify for as many races as possible. She was sure she was already fitter than many of the other kids who flopped down breathless when Mr. Ellis allowed a short rest. She decided that beginning today she would give up riding the school bus and would build up her **stamina** by running to and from school.
>
> —Dorothy Perkyns, *Last Days in Africville*

WORD ORIGIN *Stamina* comes from the Latin word *stāmina*, which is the plural of the Latin noun *stāmen*, "warp thread." (The *warp* of a fabric consists of the threads that run lengthwise in a woven fabric, crossed at right angles by the filler threads, called the *woof*.) How did Latin *stāmina*, "warp threads," become English *stamina*, "the power to resist fatigue"? In part, because a person's ability to keep going can be likened to the tightness and quality of the weave of a cloth, which determines how strong it is.

The ancient Greeks and Romans believed that three goddesses, called the Fates, spun out a thread—the "thread of life"—that determined how long a person would live. The quality of the material from which the goddesses spun the thread would determine the nobility and strength of the person's character. This belief contributed to the use of *stamina* to mean "endurance."

86 subside (səb-sīd′)

verb

To become less active, intense, or agitated; abate.

> The camp was a good one, and they stayed more days than Maroo could count, living on fish, hares, and the green food they found in the woods. Full summer came. The bitter winds **subsided**; there were no more snow showers, and the last patches of snow melted away.
>
> —Ann Turnbull, *Maroo of the Winter Caves*

> "We'll have to take care of Dragon," said Justin.
> "Yes," said Mr. Ages, "and with this leg I can't do it. I'd never make it to the bowl, much less back again."
> Mrs. Frisby, looking at their baffled faces, felt her delight **subsiding**. Obviously something was wrong.
>
> —Robert C. O'Brien, *Mrs. Frisby and the Rats of NIMH*

WORD ORIGIN *Subside* comes from Latin *subsīdere*, "to settle down." Latin *subsīdere* is a compound made up of the Latin prefix *sub-*, meaning "down, under," and the Latin verb *sīdere*, "to sit down, come to rest." Latin *sīdere* is also the source of other verbs in English relating to the notion of "coming to rest," such as *reside*.

87 swagger (swăg′ər)

verb

To walk in a way that makes it look as if you think you are important or very confident; strut.

> The front door of Tito's building opened, and a stocky man filled it. He put his thumbs in his belt and looked from side to side. Then he hunched his shoulders twice and came down the stairs. Jamal watched him **swagger** down the street.
>
> —Walter Dean Myers, *Scorpions*

WORD ORIGIN *Swagger* first appeared in the 1500s, and was probably made by adding the frequentative suffix -*er* to the verb *swag* (less common nowadays than *swagger*), meaning "to lurch or sway." A frequentative suffix is a suffix that adds a notion of repetition or frequent occurrence to a word. Another common frequentative suffix in English is -*le,* as in verbs like *sparkle* and *waddle,* and this suffix is discussed in the Word Origin note for *jostle* in this book. The verb *swag* is probably of Scandinavian origin and may ultimately be related to the English verb *sway.*

88 swarm (swôrm)

noun

A large number of insects or other small creatures, especially when in motion.

> As if to emphasize his thoughts the mosquitos—with the fire gone and protective smoke no longer saving him—came back in thick, nostril-clogging **swarms**. All that was left was the hatchet at his belt. Still there. But now it began to rain and in the downpour he would never find anything dry enough to get a fire going.
>
> —Gary Paulsen, *Hatchet*

WORD ORIGIN *Swarm* is a word that Modern English has inherited from Old English by way of Middle English. The Old English spelling of the word was *swearm*. In Old English, the word referred specifically to bees, which played a vital role in the medieval world, as they were the source of honey for sweetening food and beeswax for candles.

When a bee colony living in a hive becomes sufficiently large, the old queen and many of the other bees in the hive fly off in a swarm to find a place to start a new hive. Young queens (the old queen's daughters) are left behind and many of them may fly off with swarms, too. In medieval times, beekeepers started new hives by capturing swarms as they emerged from the old hives and then putting them in conical containers made of straw, called *skeps*, where the swarm would start a new hive.

⭐ 89 tactic (tăk′tĭk)

noun

An action that is planned to achieve a goal.

> I challenged him to a game of one on one. We flipped a penny for first outs. Ray won the toss, but I wouldn't let one little thing ruin a perfect day. He took the ball and backed me toward the hoop, dribbling side to side, his usual **tactic**.
>
> —David Patneaude, *Thin Wood Walls*

WORD ORIGIN *Tactic* comes from the Greek word *taktikos*, meaning "pertaining to arrangement, especially of troops and forces in war." *Taktikos* is related to the Greek word *taxis*, "arrangement, order." Words derived from Greek *taxis* are common in English technical and scientific vocabulary—technical words containing the element *tax-* often have to do with the notion of ordering or arranging. For example, the word *syntax*, "the order and arrangement of elements in a sentence or a computer program," comes from the Greek word *suntaxis*, "arranging together." *Taxidermy*, "arranging skins for preservation and display," contains the Greek words *taxis*, "arrangement," and *derma*, "skin."

90 terse (tûrs)

adjective

Brief and to the point; concise.

> He did not ask, for Min preferred to work with as few words as possible. The potter would bark **terse** commands, which Tree-ear struggled to satisfy by whatever means were available to him—watching Min, watching other potters, experimenting.
>
> —Linda Sue Park, *A Single Shard*

WORD ORIGIN *Terse* comes from Latin *tersus,* "rubbed clean, polished," the past participle of the Latin verb *tergēre,* "to rub clean, polish." Like us today, the Romans described writing that was free of wordiness as "polished."

91 translucent (trăns-loo′sənt)

adjective

Allowing light to pass through, but blurring it so that images cannot be seen clearly.

> It was about the same temperature whether I was inside or outside the barn. We had done our best to repair the holes in the roof, but there were still one or two little leaks that dribbled all the time. We had no spare money to replace the broken panes of glass in the windows, but we did the next best thing by taping some heavy paper over the holes and oiling the paper so it became **translucent**. It helped cut the wind down some but still let in the light.
>
> —Laurence Yep, *Dragonwings*

WORD ORIGIN *Translucent* comes from Latin *trānslūcēns*, the present participle of the Latin verb *trānslūcēre*, "to shine through." Latin *trānslūcēre* is a compound of the Latin prefix *trāns-*, "through," and the Latin verb *lūcēre*, "to shine." *Lūcēre* is the source of many other English words that have to do with the notion of brightness or shining and that contain the word-element *luc-*. One example is the English adjective *lucid*, "easily understood" or "thinking clearly." A lucid explanation is one in which the meaning shines through clearly, so to speak. Other English words from Latin *lūcēre* include *elucidate*, "to make clear," and *pellucid*, "perfectly clear" (often used to describe writing).

uncanny (ŭn-kăn′ē)

adjective

1. Arousing wonder and fear, as if supernatural; eerie. **2.** Mysterious or impossible to explain; strangely out of the ordinary.

> The nights were comfortless and chill, and they did not dare to sing or talk too loud, for the echoes were **uncanny**, and the silence seemed to dislike being broken—except by the noise of water and the wail of wind and the crack of stone.
>
> —J. R. R. Tolkien, *The Hobbit*

> I've found it doesn't pay to lie to Paul. He has an **uncanny** ability to discover the truth on his own.
>   Not, of course, that it means what I tell him is the strictest truth. I just don't practice a policy of full disclosure where Paul Slater is concerned. It seems safer that way.
>
> —Meg Cabot, *Twilight*

WORD ORIGIN The meaning of the prefix *un-* in *uncanny* is clear—it means "not"—but what exactly does the *canny* mean? The *canny* in *uncanny* is actually the same word *canny* that is still used today with the meaning "careful and shrewd." This word is associated especially with Scotland and the Scots and was probably created in the Scottish dialect of English by adding the adjective suffix *-y* (as in *fishy* from *fish* or *rosy* from *rose*) to the noun *can,* "knowledge, know-how, skill." This Scottish noun *can*, "knowledge," is actually just the verb *can*, "to be able," used as a noun. (If you *can* do a job, you *know* the things necessary to do it.)

The original meaning of *canny* was simply "knowing" and "careful," but it also developed other, related meanings such as "safe to deal with" and "lucky." Something that was "not safe to deal with" was uncanny, and *uncanny* eventually came to be applied to a specific category of things considered to be unsafe—the supernatural world.

93 unsightly (ŭn-sīt′lē)

adjective

Not pleasant to look at; unattractive.

> All day, the elders behaved unnaturally in her presence. No unintended slights, quick nods, easy smiles, teasing remarks or harsh words. They were so kind, *too* kind. Bandit felt as if she had sprouted a second head, and they were all determined to ignore politely the **unsightly** growth.
>
> —Bette Bao Lord, *In the Year of the Boar and Jackie Robinson*

WORD ORIGIN The word *unsightly* is a compound of the prefix *un-*, meaning "not," the word *sight*, meaning "the ability to see" or "the act of seeing," and the suffix *-ly*, which makes adjectives from nouns (such as *bodily* from *body*). *Unsightly* first began to become common in the 1500s.

94 versatile (vûr′sə-təl *or* vûr′sə-tīl′)

adjective

Having varied uses or functions.

> She had built a house of sod, like the summer homes of the old Eskimos. Each brick had been cut with her *ulo*, the half-moon shaped woman's knife, so **versatile** it can trim a baby's hair, slice a tough bear, or chip an iceberg.
>
> —Jean Craighead George, *Julie of the Wolves*

WORD ORIGIN *Versatile* comes from the Latin adjective *versātilis,* "capable of turning around." Something that is versatile can be turned to another purpose. *Versātilis* comes from the Latin verb *versāre,* "to turn." *Versāre* is also the source of many other English words that have to do with the notion of turning around or away and that contain the word-element *vers-*. These include *aversion,* "an intense dislike or desire to avoid," *reverse,* "to turn back, turn around," and even the noun *verse,* "a line or group of lines in a poem"—a verse is a "turn of phrase" that the poet has made, so to speak.

95 vigilant (vĭj′ə-lənt)

adjective

Watching out for danger or something that might go wrong; watchful.

> "You are not paid to be idle," the captain often declared, and he, setting an example, was never slack in *his* duty. Even at our teas, he was **vigilant**—again, so like my father—and patiently examined me as to what I had seen, heard, or even thought—always ready with quick and wise correction.
>
> —Avi, *The True Confessions of Charlotte Doyle*

> ⭐ WORD ORIGIN *Vigilant* comes from the Latin word *vigilāns,* the present participle of the Latin verb *vigilāre,* "to be watchful." *Vigilāre* itself comes from the Latin word *vigil,* meaning "awake" and "watchful." The English word *vigil,* "the act of staying awake during normal sleeping hours, often to pray" comes from the related Latin word *vigilia,* "wakefulness."

96 vulnerable (vŭl′nər-ə-bəl)

adjective

Capable of being harmed, damaged, or injured.

> The last major pieces of construction in both castle and town defense were the gatehouses. Because these were the most **vulnerable** parts of the walls, they were designed and built with great care.
>
> —David Macaulay, *Castle*

> ⭐ WORD ORIGIN *Vulnerable* comes from the Latin verb *vulnerāre,* "to wound, injure." *Vulnerāre* comes from the Latin noun *vulnus,* "wound, injury."

⭐ 97 waft (wäft *or* wăft)

verb

To float easily and gently on the air; drift.

> The smell of soup **wafted** in Despereaux's direction. He put his nose up in the air. His whiskers trembled.
>
> —Kate DiCamillo, *The Tale of Despereaux*

WORD ORIGIN The verb *waft* first appeared in English around the year 1500. At first, it was used of ships to mean "to sail in a convoy." It was also used of ships to mean "to convey something over the water." By extension, it came to be used of the wind carrying a fragrance, and the verb developed its modern meaning "to float gently on the air."

The origin of the verb *waft* is uncertain, but it may have been created by removing the *-er* from an earlier word, *wafter*. A *wafter*, also spelled *waughter*, was an armed ship defending a convoy of ships in the 15th, 16th, and 17th centuries. The word *wafter* was interpreted as being a noun formed from a verb *waft* with a suffix *-er*. Since the word *wafter* meant "a ship moving as part of a convoy," then (people thought) *waft* should mean "to move in a convoy."

The word *wafter* itself probably comes from the Dutch word *wachter*, literally meaning "guard," from the word *wachten*, "to wait, expect, stand guard." This Dutch verb is related to the English verb *watch*, "to wait and look expectantly."

98 **waver** (wā′vər)

verb

1. To move unsteadily back and forth. **2.** To hesitate or be unable to make a decision; vacillate.

> It was already dusk on the deep pathway under the overhanging branches, and her eyes were beginning to play tricks on her as the moving leaves **wavered** and shifted in the uncertain light. There was one old stump covered with ivy at the top of the bank that looked exactly like a hooded figure in a green cloak, leaning forward to listen.
>
> —Elizabeth Marie Pope, *The Perilous Gard*

> She had walked over to Black Sand's stall and he followed her, still undecided as to what he should say and hating himself for his indecision. Always before he had been positive in his decisions and he had no use for those who **wavered** in making up their minds. Was this too part of his training— black was black and white was white, with no shading, no time for doubt or understanding or compassion?
>
> —Walter Farley, *The Black Stallion and the Girl*

> WORD ORIGIN The word *waver* has been in English since Middle English times. It was probably created from the verb *wave* by adding the frequentative suffix *-er*. A frequentative suffix is added to a verb to lend a sense of repetition or frequent occurrence to the verb's meaning. For more on frequentatives, see the Word Origin notes at *jostle* and *swagger*.

---

verb

To wear away or change, as in color or surface texture, by exposure to the wind, rain, and other conditions of the atmosphere.

The Killburn houses, sheds and barns were grouped to form an enclosure. This compound was in no way extraordinary to look at, at first sight. The sheds and barns were **weathered** silver, sagging and almost shapeless.

—Virginia Hamilton, *M. C. Higgins, the Great*

He was old, with fairly long dark hair, and only a whisper of a black mustache. A shadow of a rough beard was just beginning to grow, black and gray, salt and pepper, the stubble from a few days without a razor. His face was weathered, and deep lines ran across it like the ever-changing channels of the river in the valley below. It wasn't a face forged simply by age, but a face that had been exposed too long in a land where time is measured not by the slow ticking hands of clocks, but by the quiet changing of seasons. It was a face **weathered** by erosion, like canyons or deserts.

—John Smelcer, *The Trap*

WORD ORIGIN *Weather* is a word that Modern English has inherited from Old English. *Weather* was originally a noun, but in later Middle English times it came to be used as a verb too, with meanings like "to air out" and "to expose to the weather." The Old English spelling of *weather* was *weder,* and Old English *weder* comes from a prehistoric word root *wē-,* meaning "to blow." The English word *wind* comes from the same root.

Reminded of the time, Kit leaped up and shook out her skirts.

"I must go back," she said hastily. "I must have been gone for hours."

The woman peered up at her. Her eyes, almost lost in the folds of leathery wrinkles, had a humorous gleam. A toothless smile crinkled her cheeks.

"Thee better not go back looking so," she advised. "Whatever it is, thee can stand up to it better with a bit of food inside. Come along, 'tis no distance at all."

Kit **wavered**. She was suddenly ravenous, but more than that, she was curious.

—Elizabeth George Speare, *The Witch of Blackbird Pond*

100 zeal (zēl)

noun

Great enthusiasm for or devotion to a cause, ideal, or goal.

> Cheers for Matthias's speech rang to the rafters. Constance sprang up beside him, shouting heartily, "That's the spirit, friends! Now let's see you all back out there at your posts. We'll be wide awake this time, and heaven help any dirty rats that come marching up to Redwall this day!"
>
> With wild yells very uncharacteristic of peaceful mice, the friends seized their staves and charged out, fired with new **zeal**.
>
> —Brian Jacques, *Redwall*

WORD ORIGIN *Zeal* comes from Latin *zēlus*, "zeal (especially religious zeal)." The Latin word *zēlus* is a borrowing of the Greek word *zēlos*, "zeal." The Latin word for "zealous" was *zēlōsus*, and *zēlōsus* became *gelos* in Old French. *Gelos* was used with the meaning "showing extreme attachment to a possession, unwilling to share." Old French *gelos* was borrowed into Middle English and became the English word *jealous*. In this way, the words *zeal* and *jealousy* are ultimately related.

The 100 Words

adversary
aplomb
apprehensive
aptitude
attentive
banish
barricade
bluff
brackish
brandish
circumference
commotion
concoction
conspicuous
contortion
counter
cunning
debris
defiance
deft
destination
diminish
disdain
dismal
dispel
eavesdrop
egregious
ember
emerge
engross
exasperation
exhilarate
falter
foresight

fragrance
furtive
grueling
gusto
habitation
hasten
havoc
headway
ignite
illuminate
impending
imperious
jabber
jargon
jostle
jut
kindle
knoll
luminous
malleable
materialize
meander
meticulous
misgivings
momentum
monotonous
multitude
muster
narrate
obscure
ominous
outlandish
persistent
pertinent

potential
precipice
pristine
quell
recluse
recuperate
replenish
repugnant
restitution
sabotage
scarcity
scurry
serenity
sociable
somber
specimen
stamina
subside
swagger
swarm
tactic
terse
translucent
uncanny
unsightly
versatile
vigilant
vulnerable
waft
waver
weather
zeal